SPECTRUM®

Algebra

Grades 6–8

Published by Spectrum®
an imprint of Carson Dellosa Education
Greensboro, NC

Spectrum®
An imprint of Carson Dellosa Education
P.O. Box 35665
Greensboro, NC 27425 USA

ISBN 978-1-4838-1664-7

01-111207784

Table of Contents Algebra

Chapter 1   Algebra Basics

Chapter 1 Pretest 1
Lessons 1–5 3–8
Chapter 1 Posttest 9

Chapter 2   Integers and Equations

Chapter 2 Pretest 11
Lessons 1–6 13–18
Chapter 2 Posttest 19

Chapter 3   Factors and Fractions

Chapter 3 Pretest 21
Lessons 1–6 23–28
Chapter 3 Posttest 29

Chapter 4   Rational and Irrational Numbers

Chapter 4 Pretest 31
Lessons 1–6 33–38
Chapter 4 Posttest 39

Chapter 5   Proportion, Percent, and Interest

Chapter 5 Pretest 41
Lessons 1–6 43–48
Chapter 5 Posttest 49

Chapters 1–5 Mid-Test.. 51

Chapter 6   Expressions and Equations

Chapter 6 Pretest 55
Lessons 1–6 56–61
Chapter 6 Posttest 62

Chapter 7   Equations and Inequalities

Chapter 7 Pretest 64
Lessons 1–7 66–72
Chapter 7 Posttest 73

Table of Contents, continued

Chapter 8   Functions and Graphing

Chapter 8 Pretest 75
Lessons 1–14 77–90
Chapter 8 Posttest 91

Chapter 9   Systems of Equations

Chapter 9 Pretest 94
Lessons 1–4 96–101
Chapter 9 Posttest 102

Chapters 1–9   Final Test 104

Algebra Reference Chart 108
Table of Squares and Square Roots 109
Scoring Record for Posttests, Mid-Test, and Final Test 110
Answer Key 111

Check What You Know

Algebra Basics

Write each phrase as an algebraic expression.

	a	**b**

1. three less than x _____ n divided by seven _____

2. the product of 10 and 9 _____   five more than a _____

Write each sentence as an equation or inequality. Use n for an unknown number.

3. The product of 3 and n is 12. _____   Five less than n is seven. _____

4. Two more than n is less than 10. _____   Eighteen divided by n is six. _____

Write each of the following expressions or equations in words.

5. $7 + n$ $3n + 2 = 29$

_____   _____

Write the expression for each statement.

6. the product of 4 and the difference between 8 and 3   _____

7. 4 increased by the product of 5 and 3   _____

8. the difference between 16 and the product of 4 and 2   _____

9. the quotient of 25 and 5 increased by 3   _____

10. the product of 6 and 2 decreased by 1   _____

Complete or rewrite each equation using the property indicated.

11. Commutative: $9 + 8 =$ _____   Associative: $5 \times (3 \times 4) =$ _____

12. Identity: $91 + 0 =$ _____   Property of Zero: $72 \times 0 =$ _____

NAME _____

 Check What You Know

Algebra Basics

CHAPTER I PRETEST

Find the value of each expression.

13. $(3 + 4) \times (6 + 1)$ _____ $3 + 2 \times 3 + 4$ _____

14. $(5 \times 3) + (4 \times 7)$ _____ $(3 + 2) \times (3 + 4)$ _____

15. Write the letter of the point that represents $\frac{-3}{2}$ _____

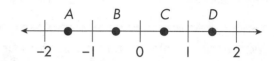

Solve each equation.

	a	**b**	**c**

16. $x - 4 = 4$ _____ $x + 3 = 5$ _____ $n - 2 = 0$ _____

17. $\frac{a}{4} = 4$ _____ $a \times 4 = 4$ _____ $\frac{m}{5} = 5$ _____

18. $y \times 20 = 30$ _____ $\frac{x}{12} = 3$ _____ $b \times 7 = 21$ _____

19. $\frac{x}{5} = 20$ _____ $n \times 5 = 25$ _____ $\frac{x}{9} = 1$ _____

SHOW YOUR WORK

Solve the problems.

20. Eva spent $48 on a shirt and a pair of pants. The pants cost twice as much as the shirt. How much did each item cost?

Let *s* stand for the cost of the shirt.

Equation: _____ $s =$ _____

The shirt cost _____. The pants cost _____.

20.

21. In Ben's office, there are 5 more women than men. There are 23 women. How many men are there?

What is the unknown number? _____

Equation: _____ $n =$ _____

There are _____ men in the office.

21.

Spectrum Algebra
Grades 6–8
2

Check What You Know
Chapter 1

Lesson 1.1 Expressions and Variables

A **variable** is a symbol, usually a letter of the alphabet, that stands for an unknown number, or quantity. a = variable

An **algebraic expression** is a combination of numbers, variables, and at least one operation. $x + 13$

An **expression** is a number phrase without an equals sign.

An **algebraic expression** is a number, variable, or combination of numbers and variables, connected by a mathematical operation like addition, subtraction, multiplication, or division. For example, in the expression $x + 5$, x is the variable.

A **numerical expression** contains only numbers: $3 + 6$

A **variable expression** contains numbers and variables: $3 + b$

All expressions express an idea.

> $5n$ means "five times n" or "five ns."
> $b - 3$ means "b decreased by 3" or "a number decreased by 3."
> In the expression $5n$, both 5 and n are **factors**.

Translate each phrase into an algebraic expression.

	a	b
1.	x increased by 2 _____	4 less than 11 _____
2.	the product of 9 and 8 _____	r added to 10 _____
3.	b divided by 5 _____	three 7s _____
4.	s decreased by 1 _____	6 more than 12 _____

Write the following expressions in words.

5. $d + 2$ _____

6. $3 \times n$ _____

Lesson 1.2   Equations and Inequalities

A **term** is a number, variable, product, or quotient in an algebraic expression. In $3a + 5$, $3a$ is a term and 5 also is a term.

The term $3a$ means $3 \times a$. The number 3 is the coefficient of a. A **coefficient** is a number that multiplies a variable. In the expression $x + 5$, the coefficient of x is understood to be 1.

An **equation** is a mathematical sentence that states that two expressions are equal. It contains an equals sign.

$2 + 5 = 7$

An **inequality** is a mathematical sentence that states that two expressions are not equal. It shows how two numbers or expressions compare to one another.

$2 + 5 > 6 \qquad 2 + 5 < 9$

Like expressions, equations and inequalities may contain only numerals, or they may also contain variables.

$2 + c = 7$

For each term below, identify the coefficient and the variable.

a   **b**

1. $3x$ coefficient _____ variable _____ $4y$ coefficient _____ variable _____

2. z coefficient _____ variable _____ $5n$ coefficient _____ variable _____

Translate each sentence into an equation or inequality. Use n for an unknown number.

3. five more than n _____   the product of n and 11 _____

Translate each sentence into an equation or inequality. Use n for an unknown number.

4. The product of n and three is greater than twenty-seven. _____

5. Ten divided by n equals two. _____

Write each equation or inequality in words.

6. $x \div 3 = 12$ _____

7. $7n + 3 < 31$ _____

Lesson 1.3 Properties

The **Commutative Properties of Addition and Multiplication** state that the order in which numbers are added or multiplied does not change the result.

$a + b = b + a$ and $a \times b = b \times a$
$2 + 3 = 5$ $5 \times 2 = 10$
$3 + 2 = 5$ $2 \times 5 = 10$

The **Associative Properties of Addition and Multiplication** state that the way in which addends and factors are grouped does not change the result.

$(a + b) + c = a + (b + c)$ and $(a \times b) \times c = a \times (b \times c)$
$(2 + 3) + 4 = 2 + (3 + 4)$ $(2 \times 4) \times 5 = 2 \times (4 \times 5)$
$5 + 4 = 2 + 7$ $8 \times 5 = 2 \times 20$
$9 = 9$ $40 = 40$

The **Identity Property of Addition** states that the sum of an addend and 0 is the addend.

$a + 0 = a$ $5 + 0 = 5$

The **Identity Property of Multiplication** states that the product of a factor and 1 is the factor.

$a \times 1 = a$ $4 \times 1 = 4$

The **Properties of Zero** state that the product of a factor and 0 is 0. They also state that the quotient of zero and any non-zero divisor is 0.

$a \times 0 = 0$ $5 \times 0 = 0$ and $0 \div a = 0$ $0 \div 5 = 0$

Name the property shown by each statement.

a **b**

1. $63 \times 1 = 63$ _____ $0 \times b = 0$ _____

2. $3 \times (5 \times 7) = (3 \times 5) \times 7$ _____ $91 + 0 = 91$ _____

3. $9 \times 8 = 8 \times 9$ _____ $0 \div 2 = 0$ _____

Complete or rewrite each equation using the property indicated.

a **b**

4. Identity: $0 + y =$ _____ Associative: $6 \times (7 \times 8) =$ _____

5. Commutative: $5 + 4 =$ _____ Properties of Zero: $0 \times 10 =$ _____

6. Associative: $7 + (b + 9) =$ _____ Commutative: $10 \times 3 =$ _____

Lesson 1.4 Order of Operations

If an expression contains two or more operations, they must be completed in a specified order. The **order of operations** is as follows:

1. Do all operations within parentheses and/or brackets (innermost first).

2. Do all multiplications and divisions, in order from left to right.

3. Do all additions and subtractions, in order from left to right.

$3 \times (4 + 5) + 6 \div 3$	Do the operation within the parentheses first.
$3 \times 9 + 6 \div 3$	Multiply and divide from left to right.
$27 + 2$	Add.
29	

Describe the steps necessary to find the value of the expression.

1. $2[5 + 6 \div 2 - (4 + 3)]$

_____

_____

_____

_____

Find the value of each expression.

	a	b
2.	$(8 - 3) \times 2$ _____	$8 - (3 \times 2)$ _____
3.	$10 - (5 + 2)$ _____	$10 - 5 + 2$ _____
4.	$(2 + 3) \times (4 + 5)$ _____	$2 + 3 \times 4 + 5$ _____
5.	$(9 \times 3) + (9 \times 2)$ _____	$[9 \times (6 - 3)] \times 2$ _____

Find the value of each expression if $a = 2$ and $b = 3$.

	a	b
6.	$5a + 2 - 1$ _____	$(b + 6) \times 4$ _____
7.	$(4a + 3b) - 2$ _____	$(3a + 3) \div b$ _____

Lesson 1.5 Coordinate Systems, Ordered Pairs, and Relations

A coordinate plane is formed by two intersecting number lines. The horizontal line is called the *x*-axis. The vertical line is called the *y*-axis. This two-axis system is called the **coordinate system.**

The coordinates of a point are represented by the ordered pair (*x*, *y*). This shows the distance the point is from the origin (0, 0), in the **domain** (the set of *x* coordinates) and the **range** (the set of *y* coordinates). A set of ordered pairs is called a **relation.**

In the graph at right, Point A is located at (4, 2). Point B is located at (−5, −3).

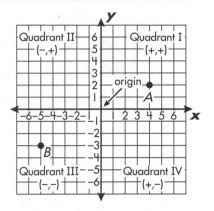

When two ordered pairs differ only by signs, the locations of the points are related by reflections across one or both axes. The coordinates of Point C differ from the coordinates of Point B by only the sign of the *x*-coordinate. So Point C, located at (5, −3), is a reflection of Point B across the *y*-axis.

Write the ordered pair for each lettered point on the grid.

1. A _____   B _____

2. C _____   D _____

3. G _____   H _____

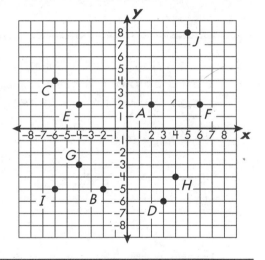

Write the ordered pair for Point *I* and Point *J* if they are reflected across the *x*-axis.

4. *I* _____   *J* _____

Plot each ordered pair on the grid. Label the points.

5. K (2, 1)   L (2, −5)

M (−2, −7)   N (−6, 6)

O (4, 6)   P (3, −2)

Q (−4, −6)   R (−7, 8)

S (5, 8)   T (−3, 2)

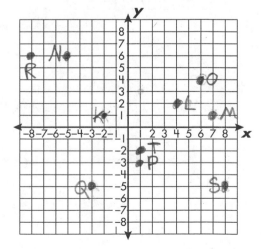

Lesson 1.5 Coordinate Systems, Ordered Pairs, and Relations

You can graph data using ordered pairs. For example, Jim has a summer job mowing lawns. He is paid $10 per hour. The amount he can earn in five hours is shown in the table below and in the graph to the right. Hours are shown on the x-axis, and dollars are shown on the y-axis.

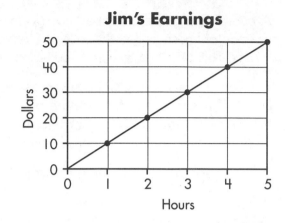

Jim's Earnings

Hours (x values)	Dollars (y values)
1	10
2	20
3	30
4	40
5	50

1. An 8th-grade class is selling tubs of cookie dough. They earn a $5 profit from each tub sold. Make a table and graph to show how much profit they will earn if they sell 100, 200, 300, and 400 tubs of cookie dough. Be sure to label the x and y axes in your graph.

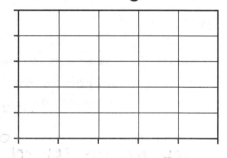

Profit from Cookie Dough Sales

Tubs (x values)	Dollars (y values)

2. Refer to the data for cookie dough sales in problem 1. How many tubs will they need to sell to earn $3,000? Represent your answer with a point on the number line. Label all values.

Check What You Learned

Algebra Basics

Write each phrase as an algebraic expression.

	a	**b**
1.	b divided by three _____	the product of seven and n _____
2.	ten less than 42 _____	seven decreased by n _____

Write each sentence as an equation or inequality. Use n for an unknown number.

3. Seven decreased by three is four. _____   Twelve divided by n is three. _____

4. Six less than x is more than ten. _____   The product of 5 and b is 20. _____

Write each of the following expressions or equations in words.

5. $b + 22$ $2b + 7 = 15$

_____   _____

Translate each phrase into an expression or an equation.

6. the sum of 3 and b _____   8 times the sum of f and 7 _____

7. product of 8 and d _____   p added to 4 equals 9 _____

Complete or rewrite each equation using the property indicated.

8. Property of Zero: $0 \div 33 =$ _____   Identity: $88 + 0 =$ _____

9. Associative: $2 + (4 + 5) =$ _____   Commutative: $6 \times 8 =$ _____

Translate each sentence into an equation. Use n for an unknown number.

10. 11 decreased by a number is 7. _____

11. 8 times a number, plus 4, is 84. _____

12. A number divided by 5 is 6. _____

Check What You Learned

Algebra Basics

Find the value of each expression.

	a	**b**
13.	$(6 + 1) \times (5 - 3)$ _____	$6 + 1 \times 5 - 3$ _____
14.	$10 - 3 + 4$ _____	$10 - (3 + 4)$ _____
15.	$(2 \times 3) + (3 \times 4)$ _____	$3 \times [10 \div (4 - 2)]$ _____

Write the ordered pair for each lettered point on Grid I.

16. A _____   B _____

17. C _____   D _____

Grid I

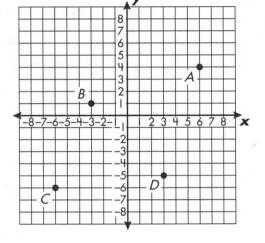

Plot each of the following ordered pairs on Grid I.

18. $E(-3, -2)$ $F(-5, 4)$

   $G(6, -2)$ $H(2, 7)$

Use Grid I to answer the following.

19. Write the ordered pair for Point B
   if it is reflected across the y-axis. _____

20. Write the distance, in units, between Point B and
   new Point B after it is reflected across the y-axis. _____

Translate each phrase into an algebraic expression or an equation. Write the expressions in words.

21. subtract 8 from 3 times d _____   take away 3 from x _____

22. g minus 2 is 14 _____   z is added to 8 _____

23. $9 \div x$ _____

24. $3 \times g = 27$ _____

Check What You Know

Integers and Equations

Add or subtract.

	a	**b**	**c**	**d**
1.	$5 + 3 =$ _____	$-5 + (-3) =$ _____	$5 + (-3) =$ _____	$-5 + 3 =$ _____
2.	$5 - 3 =$ _____	$-5 - 3 =$ _____	$5 - (-3) =$ _____	$-5 - (-3) =$ _____
3.	$-3 + (-3) =$ _____	$3 + (-3) =$ _____	$-3 + 3 =$ _____	$3 + 3 =$ _____
4.	$8 + (-8) =$ _____	$-8 + (-8) =$ _____	$8 + 8 =$ _____	$-8 + 8 =$ _____

Multiply or divide.

	a	**b**	**c**	**d**
5.	$6 \div 2 =$ _____	$6 \div (-2) =$ _____	$-6 \div 2 =$ _____	$-6 \div -2 =$ _____
6.	$5 \div (-1) =$ _____	$-5 \times (-1) =$ _____	$5 \div (-5) =$ _____	$-5 \div (-5) =$ _____

Rewrite each expression using the distributive property.

	a	**b**
7.	$4 \times (6 + 7) =$ _____	$(2 \times 3) + (2 \times 5) =$ _____
8.	$6 \times (4 - 3) =$ _____	$(4 \times 8) - (4 \times 9) =$ _____

Check What You Know

Integers and Equations

Solve each equation.

	a	b	c
9.	$4 + s = 11$ _____	$t + 9 = 21$ _____	$16 = n + 12$ _____
10.	$27 - z = 4$ _____	$x - 13 = 42$ _____	$5 = 51 - b$ _____
11.	$c - 19 = 0$ _____	$r + 5 = 10$ _____	$1 = n - 10$ _____
12.	$3 \times s = 27$ _____	$t \times 9 = 81$ _____	$6a = 42$ _____
13.	$z \div 5 = 4$ _____	$72 \div c = 18$ _____	$\frac{b}{17} = 3$ _____
14.	$\frac{20}{t} = 4$ _____	$9 = \frac{x}{3}$ _____	$0 = 15d$ _____
15.	$5b + 3 = 13$ _____	$7p - 5 = 16$ _____	$\frac{r}{10} - 3 = 1$ _____

Write an equation for each problem. Then, solve the equation.

16. In Chase's art class, there are 21 students. Nine of them are girls. How many are boys?

_____ There are _____ boys in the class.

17. Garrett earns $8.00 an hour in his summer job. Each week, he earns $160. How many hours per week does he work?

_____ He works _____ hours per week.

18. The outside temperature changed -14 °F over 4 hours. If the temperature changed the same amount each hour, what was the change in temperature each hour?

The temperature change each hour was _____ °F.

Lesson 2.1 Adding and Subtracting Integers

Integers are the set of whole numbers and their opposites. Positive integers are greater than zero. Negative integers are less than zero. A negative integer is less than a positive integer. The smaller of two integers is always the one to the left on the number line.

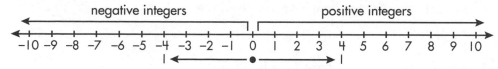

The opposite of 4 is −4. They are both 4 spaces from 0.

The sum of two positive integers is positive. The sum of two negative integers is negative.

Examples: $4 + 3 = 7$ $-4 + (-3) = -7$

To find the sum of two integers with different signs, find their absolute values. Absolute value is the distance (in units) that a number is from 0 expressed as a positive quantity. Subtract the lesser number from the greater number. The sum has the same sign as the integer with the larger absolute value.

Example: $-4 + 3 = -(4 - 3) = -1$

To subtract an integer, add its opposite.

Add or subtract.

	a	b	c
1.	$2 + 4 = $ _____	$-2 + (-4) = $ _____	$2 + (-4) = $ _____
2.	$4 - 2 = $ _____	$-4 - 2 = $ _____	$4 - (-2) = $ _____

Draw a number line to show the opposite of each number.

	a	b
3.	What is the opposite of −6?	What is the opposite of 2?

Draw a number line to represent the solution.

4. A hiker began hiking at an elevation of 3 feet below sea level. She increased her elevation by 5 feet. What was her resulting elevation?

5. The outside temperature was 2°C. The temperature decreased by 4°C. What was the resulting temperature?

Lesson 2.2   Multiplying and Dividing Integers

The product of two integers with the same sign is positive.

Examples: $5 \times 2 = 10$ $-5 \times -2 = 10$

The product of two integers with different signs is negative.

Examples: $5 \times (-2) = -10$ $-5 \times 2 = -10$

The quotient of two integers with the same sign is positive.

Examples: $10 \div 2 = 5$ $-10 \div -2 = 5$

The quotient of two integers with different signs is negative.

Examples: $10 \div (-2) = -5 - 10 \div 2 = -5$

Multiply or divide.

	a	b	c
1.	$4 \times 3 =$ _____	$-5 \times 7 =$ _____	$9 \times (-4) =$ _____
2.	$15 \div 5 =$ _____	$20 \div (-5) =$ _____	$-10 \div 2 =$ _____
3.	$-9 \times 8 =$ _____	$7 \times (-6) =$ _____	$-4 \times (-9) =$ _____
4.	$8 \div (-1) =$ _____	$-16 \div 4 =$ _____	$25 \div (-5) =$ _____
5.	$17 \times (-3) =$ _____	$-7 \times (-1) =$ _____	$9 \times (-12) =$ _____
6.	$72 \div (-4) =$ _____	$-56 \div 8 =$ _____	$-77 \div (-7) =$ _____
7.	$-4 \times (-5) =$ _____	$-5 \times 10 =$ _____	$-8 \times (-9) =$ _____
8.	$12 \div (-4) =$ _____	$32 \div 8 =$ _____	$16 \div 8 =$ _____

Simplify each algebraic expression.

9. Tam answered 4 questions incorrectly on a test. For each incorrect answer, 3 points were deducted from a perfect score of 100. What was Tam's score?

_____

10. Lin had $80 in her savings account. She used her debit card to make 3 purchases of $30 per purchase. How much was left in Lin's savings account?

_____

Lesson 2.3 The Distributive Property

The **distributive property** combines the operations of addition and multiplication.

It states that: $a \times (b + c) = (a \times b) + (a \times c)$

$$3 \times (2 + 5) = (3 \times 2) + (3 \times 5)$$

$$3 \times 7 = 6 + 15$$

$$21 = 21$$

It also means that $a \times (b - c) = (a \times b) - (a \times c)$

The distributive property helps simplify algebraic expressions. To simplify an algebraic expression:

1. Remove parentheses, using the distributive property.

2. Combine like terms. A **term** is a number, variable, or the product of a number and variable(s) in an algebraic expression. In the expression $1 + 2x + 3y + 4x + 5$, $2x$ and $4x$ are like terms. Also, 1 and 5 are like terms because they are both constants, which are terms that contain only a number.

Example:	Simplify $2(4x - 5) - 3(6x + 5)$.	Factor $6 + 10$
	$2(4x) - 2(5) - 3(6x) - 3(5)$	$(2 \times 3) + (2 \times 5)$
	$8x - 10 - 18x - 15$	$2 \times (3 + 5)$
	$-10x - 10 - 15$	
	$-10x - 25$	

Rewrite each expression using the distributive property.

	a	**b**
1.	$5 \times (3 + 4) =$ _____	$(3 \times 4) + (3 \times 6) =$ _____
2.	$15 \times (7 - 4) =$ _____	$(6 \times 5) - (5 \times 7) =$ _____
3.	$(15 + 9) =$ _____	$10x + 15 =$ _____

Simplify each algebraic expression.

4. $3(7a + 8) - 4(3a - 2)$ _____

5. $b(9 - 2) + 6(2 - b)$ _____

Lesson 2.4 Solving Addition and Subtraction Equations

The **addition and subtraction properties of equality** state that when the same number is added to both sides of an equation, the two sides remain equal:

$4 + 17 = 21$ $\quad\quad$ $4 + 17 + 5 = 21 + 5$ $\quad$ $26 = 26$

When the same number is subtracted from both sides of an equation, the two sides remain equal:

$32 = 16 + 16$ $\quad\quad$ $32 - 4 = 16 + 16 - 4$ $\quad$ $28 = 28$

Use these properties to solve equations.

$a + 3 = 14$ $\quad\quad\quad$ $b - 11 = 6$

$a + 3 - 3 = 14 - 3$ $\quad$ $b - 11 + 11 = 6 + 11$

$a = 11$ $\quad\quad\quad\quad$ $b = 17$

Solve each equation.

	a	b	c
1.	$8 + m = 13$ _____	$q + 7 = 15$ _____	$13 + b = 24$ _____
2.	$21 - c = 2$ _____	$61 - s = 30$ _____	$x - 5 = 5$ _____
3.	$34 - z = 0$ _____	$n - 41 = 60$ _____	$b - 12 = 1$ _____
4.	$22 = 10 + b$ _____	$5 = 23 - p$ _____	$11 = n + 5$ _____

Write an equation for each problem. Then, solve the equation. Explain whether your answer is reasonable.

5. Alicia baked 6 batches of cookies. 2 batches were peanut butter, 1 batch was oatmeal, and the rest were chocolate chip. How many batches were chocolate chip?

_____ Alicia baked _____ chocolate chip batches.

_____

6. Austin has 15 CDs, which is 3 less than his sister has. How many CDs does his sister have?

_____ His sister has _____ CDs.

_____

Lesson 2.5 Solving Multiplication and Division Equations

The **multiplication and division properties of equality** state that when each side of the equation is multiplied by the same number, the two sides remain equal.

$3 + 4 = 7$ $\qquad (3 + 4) \times 5 = 7 \times 5$ $\qquad 35 = 35$

When each side of the equation is divided by the same number, the two sides remain equal.

$2 \times 6 = 12$ $\qquad \frac{(2 \times 6)}{3} = \frac{12}{3}$ $\qquad 4 = 4$

Use these properties to solve equations.

$3 \times n = 15$ $\qquad\qquad n \div 6 = 8$

$3 \times \frac{n}{3} = \frac{15}{3}$ $\qquad\qquad n \div 6 \times 6 = 8 \times 6$

$n = 5$ $\qquad\qquad\quad n = 48$

Solve each equation.

	a	**b**	**c**
1.	$4 \times b = 12$ _____	$p \times 12 = 36$ _____	$7a = 35$ _____
2.	$m \div 11 = 2$ _____	$42 \div q = 6$ _____	$\frac{s}{13} = 2$ _____
3.	$\frac{100}{t} = 5$ _____	$0 = c \times 21$ _____	$49 = 7 \times d$ _____
4.	$3 = \frac{r}{4}$ _____	$\frac{9}{z} = 1$ _____	$4k = 120$ _____

Write an equation for each problem. Then, solve the equation.

5. Sabrina spent $6.25 for drinks for her friends. If each drink cost $1.25, how many drinks did she buy?

_____ She bought _____ drinks.

6. Luis has 3 times as many comic books as his best friend Orlando. If Luis has 12 comic books, how many does Orlando have? Explain whether your answer is reasonable.

_____ Orlando has _____ comic books.

_____

Lesson 2.6 Writing and Solving Two-Step Equations

Some problems with variables require more than one step to solve. Use the properties of equality to undo each step and find the value of the variable.

$2n - 7 = 19$

First, undo the subtraction by adding:

$2n - 7 + 7 = 19 + 7 \qquad 2n = 26$

Then, undo the multiplication by dividing:

$\frac{2n}{2} = \frac{26}{2} \qquad n = 13$

$\frac{n}{3} + 5 = 11$

First, undo the addition by subtracting:

$\frac{n}{3} + 5 - 5 = 11 - 5 \qquad \frac{n}{3} = 6$

Then, undo the division by multiplying:

$\frac{n}{3} \times 3 = 6 \times 3 \qquad n = 18$

Many word problems require two steps to solve.

Example: Maria bought three books and spent $48.15, including sales tax of $3.15. Each book cost the same amount. How much did each book cost?

$3x + 3.15 = 48.15 \qquad 3x = 45 \qquad x = 15$

Find the value of the variable in each equation.

	a	b	c
1.	$3b + 4 = 13$ _____	$\frac{n}{4} - 2 = 2$ _____	$12p - 10 = 26$ _____
2.	$\frac{s}{4} + 6 = 9$ _____	$13 + \frac{a}{9} = 14$ _____	$7r + 3 = 31$ _____
3.	$\frac{x}{5} - 1 = 0$ _____	$5 = 2d - 5 =$ _____	$23 = 2t + 1$ _____

Write an equation for each problem. Then, solve the equation.

4. Kendra lost $\frac{1}{2}$ of her allowance, but her mother gave her 4 more dollars. Now she has $9. How much was her allowance?

_____ Her allowance was _____.

5. Maria, Drew, and Justin all took part in a walk-a-thon. Together, they walked 9 miles. Justin walked 3 miles. Maria walked twice as far as Drew. How many miles did Drew walk?

_____ Drew walked _____ miles.

Check What You Learned

Integers and Equations

Add or subtract.

	a	**b**	**c**	**d**

1. $13 + 11 =$ _____ $-13 + (-11) =$ _____ $13 + (-11) =$ _____ $-13 + 11 =$ _____

Represent your answer with a point on a number line.

2. An elevator began on the 9th floor. It went down 7 floors. Then, it went up 4 floors. On which floor did it stop?

_____

Solve the problem using a number line or an expression.

3. The temperature was 73°F at noon. The temperature then changed by -2°F each hour for 4 consecutive hours. What was the resulting temperature?

_____

Multiply or divide.

4. $9 \div 3 =$ _____ $9 \div (-3) =$ _____ $-9 \div 3 =$ _____ $-9 \div -3 =$ _____

5. $6 \div (-1) =$ _____ $-6 \times (-1) =$ _____ $6 \div (-6) =$ _____ $-6 \div (-6) =$ _____

Rewrite the expression using the distributive property and a common factor.

6. $27x + 24x$ _____

7. $0.5n + 2.5$ _____

Simplify each algebraic expression.

8. $2(4a + 3) + 3(5a + 4)$ _____

9. $6(b + 8) - 9(3b - 4)$ _____

10. $7(3c - 2) + 4(4 - c)$ _____

Check What You Learned

Integers and Equations

Solve each equation.

	a	**b**	**c**
11.	$5 + t = 13$ _____	$s + 8 = 26$ _____	$31 = b + 27$ _____
12.	$42 - x = 29$ _____	$n - 9 = 22$ _____	$4 = 63 - z$ _____
13.	$r - 11 = 0$ _____	$c + 7 = 0$ _____	$2 = a - 9$ _____
14.	$5 \times t = 40$ _____	$s \times 8 = 48$ _____	$3b = 36$ _____
15.	$x \div 6 = 5$ _____	$81 \div n = 9$ _____	$\frac{z}{13} = 4$ _____
16.	$\frac{15}{r} = 3$ _____	$7 = \frac{c}{4}$ _____	$0 = 11a$ _____
17.	$4t + 2 = 22$ _____	$6s - 3 = 21$ _____	$\frac{b}{12} - 0 = 1$ _____

Write an equation for each problem. Then, solve the equation.

18. Jeremy has a balance of $-\$54$ in his account. He earns $9 per hour working at a photo lab. How many hours will he need to work in order for his balance to be zero?

_____ He will have to work _____ hours before he has a zero balance.

19. Nora spent $33 for 3 new T-shirts. If each T-shirt is the same price, how much did each T-shirt cost? Explain whether your answer is reasonable.

_____ Each T-shirt costs _____.

_____

_____

20. Trent had $20 to spend on 5 notebooks. After buying them, he had $7.50 left. If each notebook is the same price, how much did each notebook cost? Explain whether your answer is reasonable.

_____ Each notebook cost _____.

_____

_____

Check What You Know

Factors and Fractions

Find the greatest common factor of the two numbers.

	a	b	c
1.	12, 39 _____	18, 81 _____	14, 70 _____
2.	15, 20 _____	12, 36 _____	72, 60 _____
3.	65, 39 _____	95, 76 _____	96, 112 _____

Find the prime factorization of each number below.

4.	52	98	108
	_____	_____	_____

Write each number in scientific notation.

5.	0.0042 _____	420 _____	42,000 _____
6.	600,000 _____	700 _____	90 _____

NAME _____

Check What You Know

Factors and Fractions

Simplify each algebraic fraction. If the fraction is already in simplest form, write *OK*.

          a   **b**

8. $\dfrac{b^3}{ab^2} = $ _____ $\dfrac{6x}{12x^2} = $ _____

9. $\dfrac{9s}{14r} = $ _____ $\dfrac{100c^2}{10c} = $ _____

Use exponents to answer the question below.

10. If Serena puts $1,000 in a savings account that pays 2% interest compounded annually, how much money will she have in the account after 10 years? (Hint: To find the amount of money after 1 year, multiply by 1.02.)

She will have $ _____ in the account after 10 years.

Simplify each expression. Write each as an exponential expression.

          a   **b**

11. $3^2 \times 3^3$ _____ $5^5 \times 5^4$ _____

12. $6^{-2} \times 6^{-3}$ _____ $4^2 \times 4^{-4}$ _____

Solve each problem.

13. A store has hats for $9 each on a square table. The table is covered in hats and each hat uses 1 square foot of space. If the table is 5 feet square, how much would all the hats on the table cost?

The total cost of the the hats would be _____ .

14. A cube-shaped tank has edge lengths of $\frac{1}{2}$ foot. Sheldon used the expression $s^3 = V$ to find the volume. What was the volume of the tank?

The volume was _____ cubic foot.

Lesson 3.1 Prime Factorization and Greatest Common Factor

A **factor** is a divisor of a number. For example, 3 and 4 are both factors of 12. A **common factor** is a divisor shared by two or more numbers. The **greatest common factor** is the largest common factor shared by the numbers.

To find the greatest common factor of 32 and 40, list all of the factors of each.

$$32 \left< \begin{matrix} 1 \times 32 \\ 2 \times 16 \\ 4 \times 8 \end{matrix} \right> 1, 2, 4, 8, 16, \text{ and } 32 \qquad 40 \left< \begin{matrix} 1 \times 40 \\ 2 \times 20 \\ 4 \times 10 \\ 5 \times 8 \end{matrix} \right> 1, 2, 4, 5, 8, 10, 20, \text{ and } 40$$

The greatest common factor is 8.

A **prime number** is any number greater than 1 that has only two factors, itself and 1. (Examples: 2, 3, 5, 7) A **composite number** has more than two factors. For example, 4 has three factors: 1, 2, and 4. A composite number can be written as a product of prime numbers. This is called the **prime factorization** of the number. For example, the prime factorization of 45 is 3, 3, 5. A factor tree like the ones to the right can help determine the prime factorization of a number.

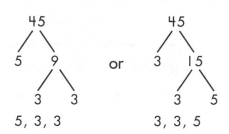

List the factors of each number below. Then, list the common factors and the greatest common factor.

	Factors	**Common Factors**	**Greatest Common Factor**
1.	9 _____	_____	_____
	15 _____		
2.	30 _____	_____	_____
	48 _____		
3.	8 _____	_____	_____
	12 _____		
4.	6 _____	_____	_____
	18 _____		

NAME_____

Lesson 3.2 Powers and Exponents

A number multiplied by itself can be written as follows: $2 \times 2 \times 2 \times 2 = 2^4 = 16$. In the expression 2^4, the small superscript 4 is called the **exponent**, and the 2 is called the **base**. An exponent is a number that indicates repeated multiplication. It shows how many times to multiply the base, the number that is being multiplied by itself. A number that can be expressed with a base and an exponent is called a **power**. For example, 2^4 is read as "2 to the 4th power." 2^2 is read as "2 to the 2nd power" or "2 squared." 2^3 is read as "2 to the 3rd power" or "2 cubed."

A number raised to the first power (n^1) is simply itself. For example, $2^1 = 2$.

A number, other than 0, raised to the 0 power (n^0) is 1. For example, $2^0 = 1$.

When solving equations with exponents, keep in mind that the Distributive Property does not apply to exponents outside parentheses. For example, $(2 + 5)^2 = (2 + 5)(2 + 5) = 7 \times 7 = 49$. It does not equal $2^2 + 5^2$ (which is $4 + 25$, or 29).

Solve the following equations.

	a	**b**
1.	$3^2 + 2^3 =$ _____	$(4 + 2)^2 =$ _____
2.	$3^4 + 6 =$ _____	$(3 + 1)^3 =$ _____
3.	$3^4 + 3^6 =$ _____	$(9 - 3)^4 =$ _____
4.	$4^3 - 4^2 =$ _____	$5^5 + 5^2 =$ _____
5.	$12^3 - 12^2 =$ _____	$(5 - 1)^3 =$ _____
6.	$(7 + 7)^3 =$ _____	$3^3 - 5^2 =$ _____
7.	$(14 - 11)^2 =$ _____	$2^5 - 10 =$ _____
8.	$8^5 + 8^3 =$ _____	$n + 7^2 = 50$ _____

Spectrum Algebra
Grades 6–8
24

Lesson 3.2
Factors and Fractions

Lesson 3.3 Simplifying Algebraic Fractions

A fraction is simplified, or reduced to lowest terms, when its numerator and denominator have no common factors other than 1. To simplify a fraction, divide the numerator and denominator by their greatest common factor.

Example: $\dfrac{60}{80} = \dfrac{(60 \div 20)}{(80 \div 20)} = \dfrac{3}{4}$

Algebraic fractions can also be simplified. Algebraic fractions are fractions with variables in the numerator and/or denominator.

Example: $\dfrac{12a^2}{15a} = \dfrac{(12a^2 \div 3a)}{(15a \div 3a)} = \dfrac{4a}{5}$

Simplify each algebraic fraction. If the fraction is already in simplest form, write *OK*.

	a	**b**
1.	$\dfrac{x^4}{x^2} =$ _____	$\dfrac{m^4}{n^2} =$ _____
2.	$\dfrac{7x}{5x^2} =$ _____	$\dfrac{mn^4}{n^2m} =$ _____
3.	$\dfrac{18t^5}{2st^2} =$ _____	$\dfrac{56f^4}{7fg} =$ _____
4.	$\dfrac{3a^5}{5b^2} =$ _____	$\dfrac{ab^5}{ab^5} =$ _____
5.	$\dfrac{4t^5u}{24tu} =$ _____	$\dfrac{cb^4}{3cb^2} =$ _____
6.	$\dfrac{9x}{18x^2} =$ _____	$\dfrac{14xy}{21xy^2} =$ _____
7.	$\dfrac{c^2}{c^3} =$ _____	$\dfrac{12ab}{15a^2b^2} =$ _____
8.	$\dfrac{25n^2}{55n} =$ _____	$\dfrac{7abc}{13a^2b^2} =$ _____
9.	$\dfrac{13x}{17y} =$ _____	$\dfrac{8sr}{20s} =$ _____
10.	$\dfrac{10b^2}{100b} =$ _____	$\dfrac{18p^2q^2}{81pq} =$ _____

Lesson 3.4 Multiplying and Dividing Powers

Use exponents to show how numbers with the same base are multiplied and divided:

$5^3 \times 5^3$ can be expressed as $5^{3+3} = 5^6$ because it means $(5 \times 5 \times 5) \times (5 \times 5 \times 5)$.

$10^6 \div 10^2$ can be expressed as $10^{6-2} = 10^4$ because it means
$(10 \times 10 \times 10 \times 10 \times 10 \times 10) \div (10 \times 10)$.

Rewrite each multiplication or division expression using a base and an exponent.

	a	b
1.	$(4 \times 4 \times 4) \times (4 \times 4) =$ _____	$7^2 \times 7^3 =$ _____
2.	$(8 \times 8 \times 8 \times 8) \div (8 \times 8) =$ _____	$4^9 \div 4^5 =$ _____
3.	$3^3 \times 3^5 =$ _____	$(6 \times 6) \times (6 \times 6) =$ _____
4.	$9^6 \div 9^3 =$ _____	$8 \times 8^5 =$ _____
5.	$(5 \times 5 \times 5 \times 5) \div (5 \times 5) =$ _____	$12^3 \times 12 =$ _____
6.	$5^5 \div 5 =$ _____	$10^5 \times 10^2 =$ _____
7.	$2^3 \times 2^5 =$ _____	$3^{11} \div 3^6 =$ _____
8.	$11^5 \div 11^2 =$ _____	$(2 \times 2 \times 2) \div 2 =$ _____

Use exponents to answer the questions below. Round to the nearest whole number.

9. If a town with a population of 3,000 grows by 2% per year, how large will the population be in 10 years? (Hint: To find the population after 1 year, multiply by 1.02).

The town's population will be _____ after 10 years.

10. How many times more people will there be in the town after 15 years than after 10 years?

There will be _____ times more people after 15 years.

Lesson 3.5 Negative Exponents

A **negative exponent** can be written with the base of the denominator in a fraction where the numerator is 1. The exponent then becomes positive.

5^{-3} means $\frac{1}{5^3} = \frac{1}{125} = 0.008$ 10^{-2} means $\frac{1}{10^2} = \frac{1}{100} = 0.01$

It is possible to multiply and divide numbers with positive and negative exponents that have the same base.

$5^{-3} \times 5^{-2} = 5^{-3 + (-2)} = 5^{-5}$ $4^{-3} \div 4^{-2} = 4^{-3 - (-2)} = 4^{-3 + 2} = 4^{-1}$

$6^{-4} \times 6^2 = 6^{-4 + 2} = 6^{-2}$ $8^4 \div 8^{-3} = 8^{4 - (-3)} = 8^{4 + 3} = 8^7$

Rewrite each multiplication or division expression using a base and an exponent.

	a	**b**
1.	$10^{-12} \times 10^{-4} =$ _____	$9^5 \div 9^{-3} =$ _____
2.	$2^{-3} \times 2^2 =$ _____	$6^{-5} \times 6^{-4} =$ _____
3.	$3^{-4} \div 3 =$ _____	$2^{-5} \div 2^3 =$ _____
4.	$5^{-5} \times 5^{-4} =$ _____	$7^4 \times 7^{-3} =$ _____
5.	$12^{-3} \div 12^3 =$ _____	$8^6 \div 8^{-3} =$ _____
6.	$6^{-6} \times 6^4 =$ _____	$11^{-3} \times 11^{-4} =$ _____
7.	$2^5 \times 2^{-6} =$ _____	$7^3 \div 7^{-2} =$ _____
8.	$4^{-3} \div 4^{-5} =$ _____	$12^{-4} \times 12^{-6} =$ _____

Use negative exponents to answer the questions below.

9. A dust mite is about 250 microns long. One micron equals 0.001 millimeter. How long is a dust mite in millimeters?

A dust mite is _____ millimeters long.

10. If a pinhead is about 2.5 millimeters in diameter, how much larger is the pinhead than a dust mite?

The pinhead is about _____ times larger than a dust mite.

Lesson 3.6 Scientific Notation

Scientific notation is most often used as a concise way of writing very large and small numbers. It involves writing a number between 1 and 10 multiplied by a power of 10. Any number can be written in scientific notation.

$1{,}503 = 1.503 \times 10^3$ ⏜ +3

$0.0376 = 3.76 \times 10^{-2}$ ⏜ −2

$85 = 8.5 \times 10$ ⏜ +1

Translate numbers written in scientific notation into standard form by reading the exponent.

$7.03 \times 10^5 = 703000$
Add 5 places.

$5.4 \times 10^{-4} = 0.00054$
Subtract 4 places.

Write each number in scientific notation.

	a	b	c
1.	38.4 _____	6,210 _____	0.031 _____
2.	47,165 _____	0.00076 _____	367.32 _____
3.	0.795 _____	921.5 _____	61,321 _____

Write each number in standard form.

4. $4.17 \times 10^{-5} =$ _____ $2.07 \times 10^3 =$ _____ $9.36 \times 10^{-4} =$ _____

5. $9.55 \times 10^2 =$ _____ $6.26 \times 10^{-2} =$ _____ $8.13 \times 10^4 =$ _____

6. $5.76 \times 10^{-1} =$ _____ $7.57 \times 10^5 =$ _____ $3.7 \times 10^{-3} =$ _____

Use scientific notation to answer the questions below.

7. Earth is about 384,400 kilometers from the moon. What is this distance in scientific notation?

Earth is about _____ kilometers from the moon.

8. Earth is about 150 million kilometers from the sun. What is this distance in scientific notation?

Earth is about _____ kilometers from the sun.

Check What You Learned

Factors and Fractions

Rewrite each of the following using a base and exponent.

a	**b**	**c**

1. $15 \times 15 =$ _____ $(5)(5)(5)(5)(5)(5) =$ _____ $9 \times 9 \times 9 \times 9 =$ _____

2. $17 \times 1 =$ _____ $s \times s \times s =$ _____ $q \times q \times q \times q \times q =$ _____

Rewrite each of the following in standard form.

3. $2^6 =$ _____ $13^2 =$ _____ $23^1 =$ _____

4. $4^3 =$ _____ $93^0 =$ _____ $10^4 =$ _____

Write each number in scientific notation.

5. $0.0027 =$ _____ $27 =$ _____ $2{,}700 =$ _____

6. $30 =$ _____ $0.004 =$ _____ $50{,}000 =$ _____

7. $500{,}000 =$ _____ $900 =$ _____ $0.0256 =$ _____

8. $0.0037 =$ _____ $100{,}000 =$ _____ $400 =$ _____

Write each number in standard form.

9. $6.14 \times 10^4 =$ _____ $6.14 \times 10^{-2} =$ _____ $6.14 \times 10^{-4} =$ _____

Check What You Learned

Factors and Fractions

Solve the following equations.

	a	b	c

10. $5^3 + 2^4 =$ _____ $(8 + 4)^2 =$ _____ $7^2 - 3^3 =$ _____

11. $(6 - 4)^5 =$ _____ $10^3 - 10 =$ _____ $b + 4^3 = 70$ _____

Simplify each algebraic fraction. If the fraction is already in its simplest form, write *OK*.

           a   b

12. $\frac{7p}{24q} =$ _____ $\frac{12mn}{18mn^2} =$ _____

13. $\frac{12b}{144b^2} =$ _____ $\frac{5a^2b^2c}{15ab} =$ _____

Rewrite each multiplication or division expression using a base and an exponent.

14. $8^{11} \times 8^4 =$ _____ $(3 \times 3 \times 3 \times 3 \times 3) \div (3 \times 3 \times 3) =$ _____

15. $3^{-6} \times 3^4 =$ _____ $11^6 \div 11^{-6} =$ _____

Solve each problem.

16. If Lucas puts $1,500 in a savings account that pays 3% interest compounded annually, how much money will he have in the account after 5 years? (Hint: To find the amount of money after 1 year, multiply by 1.03.)

He will have _____ in the account after 5 years.

17. A cube box measures 1 meter in length, width, and height. There are 10 decimeters in 1 meter. Use the expression $s^3 = V$ to find the volume of the box in decimeters.

The volume is _____ decimeters.

Check What You Know

Rational and Irrational Numbers

Solve each equation.

	a	**b**	**c**

1. $9 + d = 16$ _____ $y + 3 = 9$ _____ $12 + a = 27$ _____

2. $18 - b = 4$ _____ $23 - c = 21$ _____ $w - 11 = 11$ _____

3. $n + 8 = 41$ _____ $7 + m = 20$ _____ $9 + s = 9$ _____

4. $t + 18 = 5$ _____ $36 - a = 36$ _____ $15 - b = 0$ _____

Solve the following equations. Write each answer in simplest form.

5. $m + 3.4 = 7.9$ _____ $n - 6.3 = 9$ _____ $p - (-\frac{6}{7}) = \frac{13}{14}$ _____

6. $8t = \frac{1}{9}$ _____ $s \times \frac{3}{4} = -20$ _____ $-10.5r = -31.5$ _____

Solve each problem.

7. Ella has gold, silver, and copper wire for stringing beads. She has $1\frac{1}{2}$ ft. of gold wire, $2\frac{1}{3}$ ft. of silver wire, and $3\frac{3}{4}$ ft. of copper wire. How much wire does she have altogether?

She has _____ ft. of wire.

8. Green Valley Middle School wants to raise $7,500 for new equipment. If grades 6 and 7 each raise $2,450.25, how much money does grade 8 need to raise?

Grade 8 needs to raise _____.

NAME _____

Check What You Know

Rational and Irrational Numbers

Evaluate each expression.

a	b	c

1. $\sqrt{25} =$ _____ $\sqrt{9} =$ _____ $\sqrt{100} =$ _____

2. $\sqrt{\frac{4}{16}} =$ _____ $\sqrt{81} =$ _____ $\sqrt{\frac{9}{25}} =$ _____

Approximate the value of each expression.

3. The value of $\sqrt{10}$ is between _____ and _____.

4. The value of $\sqrt[3]{74}$ is between _____ and _____.

Use roots or exponents to solve each equation. Write fractions in simplest form.

a	b	c

5. $x^2 = 64$ $\sqrt{x} = 9$ $x^3 = 343$

  $x =$ _____ $x =$ _____ $x =$ _____

Compare using <, >, or =.

6. $\sqrt{\frac{4}{9}}$ _____ $\frac{2}{3}$ $\sqrt{10}$ _____ 5 $\sqrt[3]{25}$ _____ 3

Put the values below in order from least to greatest along the number line.

7. $14, \sqrt{18}, 4\pi$

Lesson 4.1 Changing Fractions to Decimals

Change $\frac{1}{5}$ to tenths.

$\frac{1}{5} = \frac{1 \times 2}{5 \times 2} = \frac{2}{10} = 0.2$

Change $\frac{1}{4}$ to hundredths.

$\frac{1}{4} = \frac{1 \times 25}{4 \times 25} = \frac{25}{100} = 0.25$

Change $\frac{1}{5}$ to hundredths.

$\frac{1}{5} = \frac{1 \times 20}{5 \times 20} = \frac{20}{100} = 0.20$

Change $3\frac{1}{250}$ to thousandths.

$3\frac{1}{250} = 3\frac{1 \times 4}{250 \times 4} = 3\frac{4}{1000} = 3.004$

Solve each problem. Write each answer as a fraction and then as a decimal.

1. To make one recipe, Lina needs $\frac{1}{4}$ cup of sugar. For another recipe, she needs $\frac{1}{2}$ cup of sugar. How much sugar does she need for both recipes?

Lina needs _____ cup of sugar.

Written as a decimal, this is _____ cup of sugar.

2. A table is $6\frac{1}{2}$ ft. long. Its tablecloth is $7\frac{3}{4}$ ft. long. How much longer is the tablecloth than the table?

The tablecloth is _____ ft. longer than the table.

Written as a decimal, this is _____ ft.

3. Alice and Samantha watered $\frac{5}{6}$ of the yard together. Samantha watered $\frac{1}{3}$ of that amount. What part of the yard did Samantha water?

Samantha watered _____ of the yard.

Written as a decimal, this is _____ of the yard.

4. Ramona sets aside $\frac{3}{4}$ of an hour for homework after school each day. How many hours does she do homework in 5 days?

Ramona does _____ hours of homework in 5 days.

Written as a decimal, this is _____ hours.

5. Anita can skate $3\frac{1}{3}$ miles in 1 hour. How far can she skate in $2\frac{1}{2}$ hours?

Anita can skate _____ miles in $2\frac{1}{2}$ hours.

Written as a decimal, this is _____ miles.

Lesson 4.2 Rational Numbers as Fractions

A number that can be written as the ratio of two integers is called a **rational number**. For example, the fraction $\frac{1}{3}$ is a rational number because it is the ratio 1 to 3. The number 2 is a rational number because it can be written as $\frac{2}{1}$, or the ratio of 2 to 1. A decimal is also a rational number because it can be written as a fraction. For example, $0.234 = \frac{234}{1,000}$.

A fraction whose numerator is greater than its denominator is called an **improper fraction**. An improper fraction can be changed to a **mixed numeral**, a number written as a whole number and a fraction. To change an improper fraction to a mixed numeral, divide the numerator by the denominator. For example, $\frac{18}{7}$ means $18 \div 7$. Because 7 divides into 18 two times with a remainder of 4, $\frac{18}{7}$ equals $2\frac{4}{7}$.

To change a mixed numeral into an improper fraction, multiply the whole number by the denominator and add the numerator. Place this number over the denominator.
For example, $4\frac{3}{5} = \frac{(4 \times 5) + 3}{5} = \frac{23}{5}$

Change the improper fractions to mixed numerals.

	a	b	c	d
1.	$\frac{23}{2} =$ _____	$\frac{17}{9} =$ _____	$\frac{29}{5} =$ _____	$\frac{71}{3} =$ _____
2.	$\frac{45}{4} =$ _____	$\frac{142}{15} =$ _____	$\frac{100}{33} =$ _____	$\frac{55}{7} =$ _____

Change the mixed numerals to improper fractions.

3.	$4\frac{1}{3} =$ _____	$5\frac{4}{9} =$ _____	$2\frac{4}{5} =$ _____	$3\frac{2}{7} =$ _____
4.	$7\frac{1}{4} =$ _____	$9\frac{5}{6} =$ _____	$6\frac{2}{9} =$ _____	$8\frac{3}{8} =$ _____

Lesson 4.3 Understanding Rational and Irrational Numbers

A **rational number** is a number that either terminates or repeats a pattern. It can be written as a fraction, $\frac{a}{b}$, where a and b are both whole number integers and b does not equal zero.

Here are some examples of rational numbers: 3, -5, $\frac{1}{3}$, $4.\overline{66}$, $\frac{5}{11}$, 3.25

An **irrational number** is any decimal that does not terminate and never repeats. These numbers are often represented by symbols.

Here are some examples of irrational numbers: $5.23143...$, $\sqrt{5}$, π

Tell if each number is *rational* or *irrational*.

	a	b	c
1.	$\frac{1}{5}$	$\sqrt{5}$	-5
	_____	_____	_____
2.	$\sqrt[3]{27}$	$\frac{1}{3}$	2.354
	_____	_____	_____
3.	$\sqrt{36}$	$3.\overline{45}$	$\frac{7}{9}$
	_____	_____	_____
4.	$\sqrt{20}$	19.294153	$-\frac{4}{5}$
	_____	_____	_____
5.	$\sqrt{15}$	π	$-\frac{7}{10}$
	_____	_____	_____

Lesson 4.4 Square and Cube Roots

The **square** of a number is that number times itself. A square is expressed as, for example, 6^2, which means 6×6, or 6 squared. The **square root** of a number is the value that, multiplied by itself, equals that number. The square root of 36 is 6. This is expressed as $\sqrt{36} = 6$.

Not all square roots of numbers are whole numbers, like 6. Numbers that have a whole number as their square root are called **perfect squares**.

The **cube root** of 27 is 3: $\sqrt[3]{27} = 3$, because $3 \times 3 \times 3 = 27$. Numbers that have a a whole number cube root are called **perfect cubes**.

The square root or cube root of any number that is not a perfect square is called a **radical number**. The symbols $\sqrt{}$ and $\sqrt[3]{}$ are called **radical signs**. When a number is not a perfect square, you can estimate its square root by determining which perfect squares it comes between. $\sqrt{50}$ is a little more than 7, because $\sqrt{49}$ is exactly 7. $\sqrt{60}$ is between 7 and 8 but is closer to 8, because 60 is closer to 64 than to 49. The same strategy can be used for cube roots.

A table of squares and square roots appears at the back of this book. Use the table to identify the square root of these perfect squares.

	a	b	c
1.	$\sqrt{9} =$ _____	$\sqrt{81} =$ _____	$\sqrt{36} =$ _____
2.	$\sqrt{25} =$ _____	$\sqrt{4} =$ _____	$\sqrt{64} =$ _____

Estimate the following square roots without looking at the table at the back of the book.

3. $\sqrt{80}$ is between _____ and _____ but closer to _____.

4. $\sqrt{27}$ is between _____ and _____ but closer to _____.

Identify the cube root.

5. $\sqrt[3]{8,000} =$ _____ $\sqrt[3]{125} =$ _____ $\sqrt[3]{343} =$ _____

6. $\sqrt[3]{8} =$ _____ $\sqrt[3]{64} =$ _____ $\sqrt[3]{1,000} =$ _____

Lesson 4.5 Comparing Rational and Irrational Numbers

Compare rational and irrational numbers by using a best guess for irrational numbers.

$\sqrt{3} < 2$ This statement is true because $\sqrt{3}$ is between 1 and 2.

$5 > \sqrt{20}$ This statement is true because $\sqrt{20}$ is between 4 and 5.

Approximate the value of an irrational number by exploring values.

The value of $\sqrt{2}$ is between 1 and 2. Look at the squares of 1.4 and 1.5.

  $1.4^2 = 1.96$ $1.5^2 = 2.25$

By looking at these squares, it is evident that $\sqrt{2}$ is between 1.4 and 1.5.

Rational and irrational numbers can be compared by approximating their value and placing them along a number line, such as the numbers $\sqrt{5}$, 2.5, $\sqrt{3}$

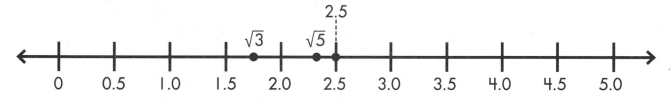

Compare using <, >, or =.

	a	**b**	**c**
1.	$\sqrt{9}$ _____ π	4.5 _____ $\sqrt{25}$	3.9 _____ $\sqrt{10}$
2.	$\sqrt{2}$ _____ 1	$\sqrt[3]{\frac{8}{27}}$ _____ $\frac{2}{3}$	1.1 _____ $\sqrt{2}$

Approximate the value of each root to the tenths place.

3. The value of $\sqrt{7}$ is between _____ and _____.

4. The value of $\sqrt{10}$ is between _____ and _____.

Put the values below in order from least to greatest along a number line.

5. π^2, 10, $\sqrt{75}$

Lesson 4.6 Solving Equations with Rational Numbers

To solve an equation with rational numbers, you must find a value that makes the variable in the equation true. To do this, use inverse operations to rearrange the equation so that the variable is alone on one side. **Inverse operations** are operations that have the opposite effect, like addition and subtraction or multiplication and division. Remember that whatever you do to one side of the equation, you must also do to the other side of the equation.

Examples:

$$a + 2.4 = 6.5$$
$$a + 2.4 - 2.4 = 6.5 - 2.4$$
$$a = 4.1$$

$$\frac{3x}{4} = \frac{2}{3}$$
$$\frac{4}{3}\left(\frac{3x}{4}\right) = \frac{2}{3}\left(\frac{4}{3}\right)$$
$$x = \frac{8}{9}$$

Solve the following equations.

	a	**b**	**c**
1.	$x + 4.1 = 6.5$ _____	$y - 7.8 = 12$ _____	$-5.4 + z = 10.2$ _____
2.	$a + \frac{2}{5} = \frac{9}{10}$ _____	$b - 1\frac{3}{4} = 4\frac{1}{4}$ _____	$c - \left(-\frac{2}{3}\right) = \frac{5}{6}$ _____
3.	$2.3m = -4.6$ _____	$-4n = 3.8$ _____	$-7.6p = -22.8$ _____
4.	$15r = \frac{1}{3}$ _____	$s \times \frac{7}{8} = -10$ _____	$\frac{t}{12} = \frac{1}{6}$ _____

Write an equation for each problem. Then, solve the equation.

5. Loreena needs $4\frac{1}{2}$ ft. of yellow yarn for a craft project. She already has $3\frac{3}{8}$ ft. How much more yarn does she need to buy?

She needs to buy _____ ft. of yarn.

6. Jaime makes $8.20 an hour in his part-time job. He made $53.30 last week. How many hours did he work?

He worked _____ hours.

Check What You Learned

Rational and Irrational Numbers

Tell if each number is *rational* or *irrational*.

	a	**b**	**c**
1.	$\frac{7}{4}$ _____	π _____	$\sqrt{99}$ _____
2.	3.635 _____	$\sqrt{77}$ _____	$\sqrt{255}$ _____
3.	5.6 _____	$\frac{1}{9}$ _____	2.756 _____

Compare the values using <, >, or =.

4. $\sqrt{36}$ _____ 6.5   1.4 _____ $\sqrt{2}$ $\frac{1}{2}$ _____ 0.55

5. 3.9 _____ $\sqrt{10}$ $\sqrt{5}$ _____ 4 $\sqrt{8}$ _____ 3

6. 1 _____ $\frac{\sqrt{16}}{25}$ $\sqrt[3]{343}$ _____ 7.2 $\sqrt[3]{6}$ _____ 2

Approximate the value to the hundredths place.

7. The value of $\sqrt{5}$ is between _____ and _____.

8. The value of $\sqrt{13}$ is between _____ and _____.

Create a number line to show each set of values in order from least to greatest.

9. π, $\sqrt{10}$, -3, $\frac{7}{4}$

Check What You Learned

Rational and Irrational Numbers

Change each of the following to a decimal as indicated.

	a	b	c

10.   Change $\frac{2}{5}$ to tenths.   Change $\frac{13}{25}$ to hundredths.   Change $\frac{43}{250}$ to thousandths.

_____   _____   _____

11.   Change $6\frac{9}{25}$ to hundredths.   Change $5\frac{49}{50}$ to hundredths.   Change $3\frac{1}{8}$ to thousandths.

_____   _____   _____

Change the improper fractions to mixed numerals and the mixed numerals to improper fractions.

	a	b	c	d

12. $\frac{25}{2} =$ _____ $\frac{13}{9} =$ _____ $\frac{51}{5} =$ _____ $\frac{22}{3} =$ _____

13. $\frac{60}{11} =$ _____ $\frac{47}{10} =$ _____ $9\frac{1}{3} =$ _____ $8\frac{1}{2} =$ _____

14. $7\frac{2}{5} =$ _____ $6\frac{5}{7} =$ _____ $5\frac{5}{8} =$ _____ $4\frac{5}{9} =$ _____

Check What You Know

Proportion, Percent, and Interest

Circle the proportions that are true. Show your work.

	a	**b**	**c**
1.	$\frac{6}{8} = \frac{12}{16}$	$\frac{3}{7} = \frac{9}{24}$	$\frac{4}{5} = \frac{20}{25}$
2.	$\frac{5}{3} = \frac{16}{9}$	$\frac{3}{5} = \frac{21}{35}$	$\frac{9}{10} = \frac{15}{20}$

Solve for n in each proportion.

3. $\frac{4}{n} = \frac{28}{35}$ _____ $\frac{2}{3} = \frac{16}{n}$ _____ $\frac{n}{9} = \frac{45}{81}$ _____

4. $\frac{11}{12} = \frac{n}{36}$ _____ $\frac{10}{n} = \frac{18}{27}$ _____ $\frac{42}{24} = \frac{7}{n}$ _____

5. $\frac{7}{5} = \frac{28}{n}$ _____ $\frac{4}{6} = \frac{n}{21}$ _____ $\frac{6}{n} = \frac{15}{20}$ _____

6. $\frac{n}{9} = \frac{14}{18}$ _____ $\frac{15}{18} = \frac{10}{n}$ _____ $\frac{n}{30} = \frac{13}{10}$ _____

7. $\frac{10}{8} = \frac{n}{24}$ _____ $\frac{11}{12} = \frac{44}{n}$ _____ $\frac{n}{2} = \frac{9}{6}$ _____

8. $\frac{12}{n} = \frac{4}{5}$ _____ $\frac{10}{14} = \frac{n}{35}$ _____ $\frac{10}{n} = \frac{25}{15}$ _____

For each fraction or decimal, write the equivalent percent form.

	a	**b**	**c**
9.	$\frac{3}{25} =$ _____	$0.01 =$ _____	$\frac{2}{5} =$ _____
10.	$4.06 =$ _____	$\frac{1}{8} =$ _____	$0.6 =$ _____

NAME _____

Check What You Know

Proportion, Percent, and Interest

Solve each problem.

11. Isabel biked 4 miles in 15 minutes. At that rate, how far will she bike in 45 minutes?

She will bike _____ miles in 45 minutes.

12. All shirts on the clearance rack are 60% off. If one of the shirts was originally $29.95, how much does it cost now?

The shirt costs $_____ now.

13. The sales tax on the purchase of a refrigerator that costs $695 is 7 percent. What is the amount of sales tax?

The amount of sales tax is _____.

14. A stove that costs $695 will be on sale next week for 28 percent off its regular price. What is the amount of savings?

The savings will be _____.

Fill in the missing information about each loan.

	Principal	Rate	Time	Compounded	Interest	Total Amount
15.	$4,000	_____	2 years	no	$320	$4,320
16.	$1,500	$6\frac{1}{2}\%$	_____	no	$292.50	$1,792.50
17.	$600	7%	4 years	no	_____	_____
18.	_____	5%	$2\frac{1}{2}$ years	no	$437.50	_____
19.	$2,000	$4\frac{1}{4}\%$	3 years	annually	_____	_____
20.	$800	2%	2 years	semi-annually	_____	_____

Lesson 5.1 Ratio and Proportion

A **ratio** is a comparison of two numbers. A ratio can be expressed as 1 to 2, 1:2, or $\frac{1}{2}$. It means that for every 1 of the first item, there are 2 of the other item. For example, 2 dollars per gallon is a ratio. For every 1 gallon you buy, you pay 2 dollars.

A **proportion** expresses the equality of two ratios. To check if a proportion is true, cross-multiply to determine if the two ratios are equal.

$\frac{4}{2} \diagup\!\!\!\diagdown \frac{2}{1}$ $\frac{4}{2} = \frac{2}{1}$ $4 \times 1 = 2 \times 2$, so it is true. $\frac{3}{4} = \frac{2}{3}$ $3 \times 3 \neq 4 \times 2$, so it is **not** true.

Circle the proportions that are true. Show your work.

	a	b	c
1.	$\frac{1}{4} = \frac{2}{8}$	$\frac{1}{3} = \frac{4}{9}$	$\frac{2}{7} = \frac{6}{21}$
2.	$\frac{9}{4} = \frac{27}{16}$	$\frac{3}{25} = \frac{12}{100}$	$\frac{4}{5} = \frac{12}{20}$

The picture, table, and graph below all illustrate the same ratio.

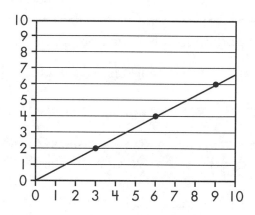

3	6	9
2	4	6

3. Which fraction expresses this ratio in simplest form? Circle the correct answer.

a. $\frac{3}{6}$ b. $\frac{3}{4}$ c. $\frac{3}{2}$

Complete the tables to solve the ratio problems. Circle your answer in the table.

4. An ice-cream factory makes 180 quarts of ice cream in 2 hours. How many quarts could be made in 12 hours?

Ice Cream	180 quarts					
Hours	2 hours	4 hours	6 hours	8 hours		

Lesson 5.2 Solving Proportion Equations

A **ratio** is a comparison of two numbers. A **proportion** expresses the equality of two ratios.

Cross-multiply to determine if two ratios are equal.

$\frac{2}{4}, \frac{3}{6}$ $2 \times 6 = 12$ $3 \times 4 = 12$ $\frac{2}{4} = \frac{3}{6}$

To find the unknown number in a proportion, first cross-multiply to make an equation. Then, divide both sides by the number with n.

$\frac{4}{5} = \frac{n}{15}$ $4 \times 15 = 5 \times n$ $60 \div 5 = 5n \div 5$

                                $60 = 5n$ $12 = n$

In proportion problems, two things change at the same rate. Example: The Longs drove 680 miles in 2 days. At that rate, how far will they drive in 5 days?

Let n equal the unknown number—in this case, how far the Longs will drive in 5 days. Set up a proportion. For example, compare the number of days to the number of miles, or the number of miles to the number of days. Whichever you choose, do the same for both sides of the proportion. Then, cross-multiply to solve.

$\frac{2}{5} = \frac{680}{n}$ or $\frac{680}{2} = \frac{n}{5}$ In each case, $n = 1,700$

Use a proportion to solve each problem.

1. Marta walked 2 miles in 28 minutes. At that rate, how far can she walk in 70 minutes?

She can walk _____ miles in 70 minutes.

2. On a map, each inch represents 20 miles. If two cities are 5 inches apart on the map, how far apart are the two cities in miles?

They are _____ miles apart.

Solve the problem by finding the unit rate.

3. Sasha can walk 6 miles in 3 hours. If she has to walk 1 mile, how long will it take her?

Sasha can walk 1 mile in _____ hour.

Determine if the pairs of ratios are equivalent. Write *yes* or *no*.

	a	b	c
4.	$\frac{1}{3}$ and $\frac{2}{6}$ _____	$\frac{1}{2}$ and $\frac{8}{16}$ _____	$\frac{9}{12}$ and $\frac{10}{12}$ _____
5.	$\frac{3}{8}$ and $\frac{7}{16}$ _____	$\frac{2}{5}$ and $\frac{4}{10}$ _____	$\frac{6}{9}$ and $\frac{12}{15}$ _____

Lesson 5.3 Understanding Percents

Percent (%) means "out of 100."

Examples: 1 percent (1%) = 0.01 = $\frac{1}{100}$.   125% = 1.25 = $1\frac{25}{100}$ = $1\frac{1}{4}$.

Use this method to change a percent to a fraction:

$$12\% = \frac{12}{100} \div \frac{4}{4} = \frac{3}{25}$$

Use this method to change a decimal to a percent:

$$0.165 = \frac{16.5}{100} = 16.5\%$$

Use this method to change a fraction to a percent:

$$\frac{5}{8} = \frac{n}{100} \quad 500 = 8n \quad 62\frac{1}{2}\% = n$$

Use this method to change a percent to a decimal:

$$49.5\% = \frac{49.5}{100} = 0.495$$

For each fraction or mixed numeral, write the equivalent percent. For each percent, write the equivalent fraction or mixed numeral.

	a	b	c
1.	20% = _____	_____% = $\frac{3}{8}$	120% = _____
2.	_____% = $2\frac{5}{8}$	82% = _____	14.25% = _____
3.	164% = _____	_____% = $\frac{7}{20}$	_____% = $\frac{4}{25}$
4.	_____% = $\frac{19}{20}$	248% = _____	_____% = $3\frac{3}{10}$

For each decimal, write the equivalent percent. For each percent, write the equivalent decimal.

	a	b	c
5.	5.75% = _____	_____% = 0.125	58% = _____
6.	_____% = 1.15	9% = _____	_____% = 0.035
7.	225% = _____	_____% = 0.005	99% = _____
8.	_____% = 0.8	_____% = 3.82	52.25% = _____

Lesson 5.4 Finding Percent

What number is $17\frac{1}{2}\%$ of 80?

$17\frac{1}{2}\%$ of 80 = 17.5% × 80

$0.175 × 80 = 14$

$17\frac{1}{2}\%$ of 80 is 14.

---

50 is what percent of 80?

$50 = n\% × 80 \quad 50 = \frac{n}{100} × 80$

$50 = 80\frac{n}{100} \quad 5,000 = 80n$

$5,000 ÷ 80 = 80n ÷ 80$

$62.5 = n \quad$ 50 is 62.5% of 80.

---

15 is 30% of what number?

$15 = 30\% × n$

$15 = \frac{30}{100} × n$

$15 = \frac{3n}{10} \quad 150 = 3n$

$50 = n \quad$ 15 is 30% of 50.

What number is 5% more than 950?

$950 + 5\%$ of $950 = 950 + (5\% × 950) =$

$950 + (0.05 × 950) = 950 + 47.50 = 997.50$

997.50 is 5% more than 950.

---

102 is what percent less than 120?

$120 - 102 = 18 \quad\quad 18 = n\%$ of 120

$18 = n × 120 \quad\quad \frac{18}{120} = n$

$0.15 = n \quad$ 102 is 15% less than 120.

Solve each problem.

1. All winter jackets are on sale for 75% off. If a jacket originally cost $90, how much does it cost now?

   The jacket now costs $_____.

2. Marcus went on a diet and now weighs 140 lb. He originally weighed 175 lb. What percent of his weight did he lose?

   He lost _____% of his weight.

3. The sales tax on the purchase of a refrigerator that costs $850 is 7 percent. What is the amount of sales tax?

   The sales tax is _____.

4. A stove that costs $500 will be on sale next week for 25 percent off its regular price. What is the amount of savings?

   The savings will be _____.

5. East Side Middle School has 1,500 students. Thirty-two percent of them are in sixth grade. How many sixth-grade students are there?

   There are _____ sixth-grade students.

Lesson 5.5 Figuring Simple Interest

Interest is the amount paid on borrowed money, or the amount earned on invested money. **Principal** is the amount borrowed or invested. Use this formula to figure simple interest:

$$interest = principal \times rate \times time \text{ (in years)}.$$

Carla got a $3,000 car loan to be paid in 2 years. The interest rate is 6%. What will the interest be at the end of the 2 years?

$$i = \$3,000 \times 0.06 \times 2 = \$360$$

Hector got a $500 loan for $1\frac{1}{2}$ years. He paid $60 in interest. What was the interest rate?

$$60 = 500 \times r \times 1.5 \quad 60 = 750r \quad \tfrac{60}{750} = r$$
$$0.08 = r \quad 8\% = r$$

Toni got a loan for 2 years. The interest rate was 6%. She paid $120 in interest. How much was the principal?

$$120 = p \times 0.06 \times 2 \quad 120 = p \times 0.12$$
$$\tfrac{120}{0.12} = p \quad \$1,000 = p$$

David got a loan for $1,700. The interest rate was 5%. He paid $212.50 in interest. What was the length of the loan?

$$212.5 = 1,700 \times 0.05 \times t$$
$$212.5 = 85t \quad 2.5 = t$$

Fill in the missing information about each loan.

	Principal	Rate	Time	Interest
1.	$5,000	_____	3 years	$750
2.	$2,500	3%	_____	$112.50
3.	$800	$5\frac{1}{2}$%	4 years	_____
4.	_____	4%	$2\frac{1}{2}$ years	$650

Solve each problem.

5. Monica got a $4,500 car loan to be paid in 3 years. The interest rate is 5%. What will the interest be at the end of the 3 years?

   The interest will be $_____.

6. Gabriel got a loan for $1\frac{1}{2}$ years. The interest rate was 4%. He paid interest of $240. How much was the principal?

   The principal was $_____.

Lesson 5.6 Figuring Compound Interest

Compound interest is interest paid on principal and interest already earned.

A savings account earns 3% interest, compounded annually. If the amount in the account is $500 at the start of the loan, how much will be in the account after 4 years?

Year 1: 500 + (500 × 0.03) = 515   Year 2: 515 + (515 × 0.03) = 530.45

Year 3: 530.45 + (530.45 × 0.03) = 546.36   Year 4: 546.36 + (546.36 × 0.03) = 562.75

The graph below shows the compounding interest.

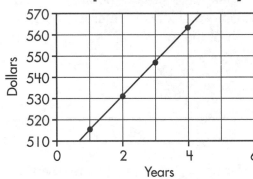

$500 with 3% Interest Compounded Annually

If interest is compounded more than once a year, divide the amount compounded each time by the number of times it is compounded annually.

For interest compounded:	Divide by:
semi-annually	2
quarterly	4
monthly	12

An account of $500 pays 5% compounded monthly. At the end of Month 1, the account will have:
$500 + ($500 × 0.05 ÷ 12) = $502.08

Find the total amount in each account after the given time. Round to cents.

	Principal	Rate	Time	Compounded	Total Amount
1.	$2,500	8%	4 years	annually	_____
2.	$3,000	$5\frac{1}{2}$%	3 years	annually	_____
3.	$1,500	$3\frac{1}{2}$%	2 years	semi-annually	_____
4.	$700	5%	1 year	quarterly	_____

Solve the problem below.

5. Elena has $500 to invest. She can put it in an account that earns 4% compounded semi-annually or in an account that earns 5% simple interest. After 2 years, how much will be in each account, including the principal?

The 4% account will have _____. The 5% account will have _____.

Check What You Learned

Proportion, Percent, and Interest

Circle the proportions that are true. Show your work.

	a	**b**	**c**
1.	$\frac{3}{2} = \frac{75}{50}$	$\frac{10}{7} = \frac{30}{21}$	$\frac{2}{5} = \frac{4}{15}$
2.	$\frac{2}{4} = \frac{7}{14}$	$\frac{7}{9} = \frac{49}{81}$	$\frac{13}{8} = \frac{39}{24}$

Determine if the pairs of ratios are equivalent. Write *yes* or *no*.

3. $\frac{4}{6}$ and $\frac{15}{18}$ _____ $\frac{1}{2}$ and $\frac{4}{8}$ _____ $\frac{3}{7}$ and $\frac{8}{10}$ _____

4. $\frac{3}{4}$ and $\frac{9}{12}$ _____ $\frac{5}{11}$ and $\frac{7}{11}$ _____ $\frac{1}{4}$ and $\frac{3}{5}$ _____

Solve each problem.

5. Three baskets of oranges weigh 120 pounds. How many pounds are in 4 baskets?

There are _____ pounds in 4 baskets.

6. There are 60 pencils in 4 pencil boxes. How many pencils are in 7 boxes?

There are _____ pencils in 7 boxes.

7. The supply store sells 4 pencils for every 5 pens. The store sold 28 pencils yesterday. How many pens did it sell?

The store sold _____ pens.

Check What You Learned

Proportion, Percent, and Interest

Solve each problem.

8. Angelina ran 2 miles in 15 minutes. At that rate, how far will she run in 1 hour?

   She will run _____ miles in 1 hour.

9. At the end of summer, all sandals are marked down by 70%. If a pair of sandals originally cost $19.50, how much will it cost at the end of summer?

   It will cost _____ at the end of summer.

10. Mr. Johnson borrowed $750 for 1 year. He has to pay 6% simple interest. How much interest will he pay?

    Mr. Johnson will pay _____ in interest.

Complete the table to solve the ratio problems. Circle your answer in the table.

11. A jet travels 650 miles in 3 hours. At this rate, how far could the jet fly in 9 hours?

Distance	650 miles		
Hours	3 hours		

Fill in the missing information about each loan.

	Principal	Rate	Time	Compounded	Interest	Total Amount
12.	$750	3%	5 years	no	_____	_____
13.	_____	6%	$\frac{1}{2}$ year	no	$90	_____
14.	$4,000	$3\frac{1}{2}$%	3 years	annually	_____	_____
15.	$500	8%	2 years	semi-annually	_____	_____

Mid-Test Chapters 1–5

Rewrite each expression using the property indicated.

a	b

1.   identity: $1 \times p =$ _____   associative: $(9 + k) + 3 =$ _____

2.   commutative: $z \times 7n =$ _____   distributive: $6w + 6x =$ _____

Underline the operation that should be done first. Then, find the value of the equation.

3. $9 + 8 \div -4 =$ _____ $4 \times (-6 + 3) + 8 \div 2 =$ _____

4. $6 + 15 \div 3 \times 2 =$ _____ $(8 - 3) \times 2 \div 8 =$ _____

5. $(2 + 6) \times (-4 - 8) =$ _____ $4 \times [11 \times (6 - 3)]$ _____

Solve each equation.

a	b	c

6. $p + 33 = 105$ _____ $k - 74 = 17$ _____ $14 \times a = 126$ _____

7. $396 \div b = 99$ _____ $84 - g = 45$ _____ $29 = y + 18$ _____

8. $0 \div 65n =$ _____ $\frac{m}{6} - 2 = 13$ _____ $31 = 4t + 3$ _____

Write an equation for each problem. Use n as the variable. Then, solve the equation.

9. Nick worked 6 hours today and earned a total of $54. What is Nick's hourly wage?

Equation _____   Nick earns _____ per hour.

10. Jack and Dion sold a total of 33 appliances for their store. Dion sold 3 less than twice as many appliances as Jack sold. How many appliances did each person sell?

Equation _____   Jack sold _____ and Dion sold _____ appliances.

Mid-Test Chapters 1–5

Write the ordered pair for each lettered point. Plot the points for the ordered pairs given.

	a	**b**	**c**
11.	W _____	X _____	Y _____

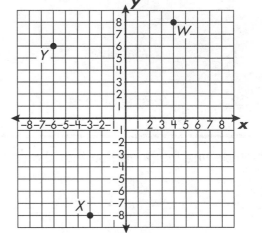

12. A $(-2, 3)$ B $(6, -4)$ C $(-5, -3)$

13. D $(5, 2)$ E $(-8, -6)$ F $(7, -2)$

Solve the following equations.

14. $6^2 - 2^3 =$ _____ $4^4 + 2^4 =$ _____ $(6 + 3)^2 =$ _____

15. $5^3 - 25 =$ _____ $(5 - 3)^3 =$ _____ $y + 2^0 = 40$ _____

Rewrite each expression using a base and an exponent.

16. $7^{-6} \times 7^3 =$ _____ $4^{-5} \times 4^{-3} =$ _____ $6^5 \div 6^{-7} =$ _____

Write each number in scientific notation.

17. 7,564 _____   0.0897 _____   32,857 _____

18. 30 _____   4,000 _____   50,000 _____

19. 600,000 _____   700 _____   90 _____

20. 40,000 _____   100,000 _____   400 _____

Mid-Test Chapters 1–5

Solve each problem. Write the answer in simplest form.

a	**b**	**c**

21. $p + 6.2 = 4.5$ _____ $\quad 4y = \frac{1}{2}$ _____ $\quad -3.2b = -12.4$ _____

22. $m \times \frac{3}{8} = -2$ _____ $\quad k - (-\frac{3}{4}) = \frac{11}{12}$ _____ $\quad -n + \frac{2}{3} = \frac{5}{6}$ _____

Write an equation for each problem. Use *n* as the variable. Then, solve the equation.

23. To make a trail mix, Terry combined $2\frac{1}{3}$ pounds of peanuts, $\frac{3}{4}$ pound of almonds, and $1\frac{1}{6}$ pounds of cashews. How much trail mix does Terry have?

Equation _____ Terry has _____ pounds of trail mix.

24. Tamika used $6\frac{1}{4}$ gallons of paint. Each room she painted took $1\frac{1}{4}$ gallons. How many rooms did she paint?

Equation _____ Tamika painted _____ rooms.

Find the value of the variable in each equation.

25. $a + 13 = 27$ _____ $\quad 2n - 2 = 10$ _____ $\quad \frac{x}{4} + 4 = 12$ _____

26. $18 - 2p = 10$ _____ $\quad \frac{n}{24} = 3$ _____ $\quad n - 33 = 19$ _____

27. $a + 12 = 25$ _____ $\quad 48 + d = 60$ _____ $\quad y + 19 = 18$ _____

28. $31 - x = 16$ _____ $\quad 11 + n = 25$ _____ $\quad m - 21 = 34$ _____

Mid-Test Chapters 1–5

Solve each problem.

29. The Jacksons' dinner cost $125. They left $21.25 for a tip. What percent did they tip?

The Jacksons tipped _____.

30. A sweater was originally $55. It is now marked down to 65% of its original price. How much is the sweater now?

The sweater now costs _____.

31. Ms. Martino's new home cost $260,000. She paid $39,000 in a down payment. What percent of the home cost did she pay in the down payment?

Ms. Martino paid _____ of the total price.

32. Skirts are 4 for $30. Marta and her sisters bought 6 skirts. How much did they pay?

They paid _____.

33. Sweaters are 3 for $50. Leslie and her mother spent $100 on sweaters. How many did they buy?

They bought _____ sweaters.

34. A machine makes 36 widgets in 20 minutes. At that rate, how many widgets will the machine make in an 8-hour day?

The machine will make _____ widgets in a day.

Fill in the missing information about each loan.

	Principal	Rate	Time	Compounded	Interest	Total Amount
35.	$2,000	_____	5 years	no	$1,250.00	$3,250
36.	$4,200	$6\frac{1}{4}$ %	_____	no	$2,100	$6,300
37.	$6,000	4%	3 years	annually	_____	_____
38.	$300	5%	2 years	semi-annually	_____	_____

Check What You Know

Expressions and Equations

Create expressions equivalent to the ones below.

1. $4(a + b)$ _____

2. $3(9a + 8b)$ _____

3. $9(x + 2y)$ _____

Solve. Write your answer in simplest form.

4. The standard size of a bin holds $2\frac{2}{3}$ gallons. The large size of that bin is $1\frac{1}{4}$ times larger. How many gallons does the large bin hold?

The large bin holds _____ gallons.

5. Diana has $3\frac{1}{4}$ bags of nuts. Each bag holds $4\frac{1}{2}$ pounds. How many pounds of nuts does Diana have?

Diana has _____ pounds of nuts.

6. Each month, Kelsey donates $\frac{1}{5}$ of her allowance to her school for supplies. Of that amount, $\frac{1}{2}$ goes to the chorus class. How much of her allowance goes to supplies for the chorus class?

_____ of her allowance goes to help the chorus classes.

Use the Distributive Property to factor each expression.

7. $32a + 56b$ _____

8. $15y + 18x$ _____

NAME _____

Lesson 6.1 Equivalent Expressions

Equivalent expressions are created by simplifying values and combining terms.

$4(6x - 5) = 24x - 20$ Multiply each value by 4 to create an equivalent expression.

$3(4^3 + 7x) = 3(64 + 7x)$ First, calculate the value of the exponents.

$3(64 + 7x) = 192 + 21x$ Then, use the distributive property to create the equivalent expression.

$t + t + t = 3t$ Use multiplication in place of repeated addition.

Create expressions equivalent to the ones below.

1. $7(4z + 8b)$ _____

2. $8(2x + 3^2)$ _____

3. $4(r + r + r + r)$ _____

4. $9(3 + 8x)$ _____

5. $4^2(3 + 6t)$ _____

6. $\frac{t + t + t}{4}$ _____

7. $2(4s^3 + 2)$ _____

8. $30(3x + 4)$ _____

9. $6(5a + 9b)$ _____

10. $9(3x + 54)$ _____

11. $7(c + c + c)$ _____

12. $9(2 + 7f)$ _____

Lesson 6.2 Factoring Expressions

Factoring expressions involves the use of the distributive property. You've learned how to use the distributive property to expand expressions:

$3(4x + 5) = (3 \times 4x) + (3 \times 5) = 12x + 15$

Because 3 is a factor of both numbers, a factored form of $12x + 15$ is $3(4x + 5)$.

By factoring, you are "pulling out" a common factor of both terms in an expression.

Many times, you are looking to find the greatest common factor (GCF) of both terms.

To factor $6a + 4b$, first look for the greatest common factor of the terms. The coefficients 6 and 4 are both divisible by 2. So, the GCF is 2.

First, determine what to multiply 2 by to get $6a$; $2 \times 3a = 6a$.

$2(3 + \underline{})$

Then, determine what to multiply 2 by to get $4b$; $2 \times 2b = 4b$.

$2(3a + 2b) = 6a + 4b$

Use the distributive property and greatest common factor to factor each expression. If the expression cannot be factored, write OK.

	a	**b**
1.	$4m + 12$ _____	$2x + 8y$ _____
2.	$9t + 18$ _____	$10v - 15w$ _____
3.	$6b - 18a$ _____	$42 + 70$ _____
4.	$14y + 35x$ _____	$m + 3n$ _____
5.	$39 + 91$ _____	$2f + 48$ _____
6.	$x - 51x$ _____	$-4s + 56$ _____
7.	$7y + 56z$ _____	$5p + 30q$ _____

Lesson 6.3 Converting Rational Numbers to Solve Problems

When solving real-world problems involving fractions, you need to first determine which operation to use. Then, you can write an expression to help you solve the problem.

For example, Joe runs $2\frac{1}{2}$ miles each day for 3 days. How many miles did he run?

To find the total number of miles ran, multiply the distance per day by the number of days. The expression would be: $2\frac{1}{2} \times 3$.

Sue ran $9\frac{3}{4}$ miles over 3 days. If she ran the same number of miles each day, how many miles did she run each day?

To find the number of miles each day, divide the distance by the number of days. The expression would be: $9\frac{3}{4} \div 3$

Sometimes, it is easier to solve equations by writing them in different ways.

A number increased by 10% can be written as:

- $n + (0.10 \times n)$
- $1.10 \times n$

A number divided by 7 equals 3 can be written as:

- $n \div 7 = 3$
- $3 \times 7 = n$

Solve each problem. Write each answer in simplest form.

1. David worked $7\frac{1}{3}$ hours today and planted 11 trees. It takes him about the same amount of time to plant each tree. How long did it take him to plant each tree?

    It took him _____ hour to plant each tree.

2. A car uses $3\frac{1}{8}$ gallons of gasoline per hour when driving on the highway. How many gallons will it use after $4\frac{2}{3}$ hours?

    It will use _____ gallons.

Write two equivalent expressions for each statement.

a	**b**
3. *a* divided by 5 equals 9	*k* increased by $\frac{1}{5}$
_____	_____
_____	_____

Lesson 6.4 Creating Expressions to Solve Problems

Write expressions to solve problems by putting the unknown number, or variable, on one side of the equation and the known values on the other side of the equation. Then, solve for the value of the variable.

Francine is making earrings and necklaces for six friends. Each pair of earrings uses 6 centimeters of wire and each necklace uses 30 centimeters. How much wire will Francine use?

Let w represent the amount of wire used. Equation: ___$w = 6 \times (6 + 30)$___

Another way of writing this expression is: $w = (6 \times 6) + (6 \times 30)$

How much wire did Francine use? ___$w = 216$ centimeters___

SHOW YOUR WORK

Solve each problem.

1. A jaguar can run 40 miles per hour while a giraffe can run 32 miles per hour. If they both run for 4 hours, how much farther will the jaguar run?

   Let d represent the distance.

   Equation: _____

   Another way of writing this is: _____

   The jaguar will run _____ miles farther.

   1.

2. Charlene sold 15 magazine subscriptions for the school fundraiser. Mark sold 17 subscriptions and Paul sold 12. How many magazine subscriptions did they sell in all?

   Let s represent subscriptions.

   Equation: _____

   Another way of writing this is: _____

   They sold _____ subscriptions in all.

   2.

3. Shara bought 3 bags of chocolate candies for $1.25 each and 3 bags of gummy bears for $2.00 each. How much did she spend in all?

   Let m represent the money spent.

   Equation: _____

   Another way of writing this is: _____

   Shara spent _____ on candy.

   3.

Lesson 6.5 Using Variables to Solve Problems

Write an equation to represent the problem, using the variable *n* for the unknown number. Then, solve for the value of the variable. Look at the following problem as an example.

George and Cindy are saving for bicycles. Cindy has saved $15 less than twice as much as George has saved. Together, they have saved $120. How much did each of them save?

Let *n* stand for the amount George has saved. What stands for the amount Cindy has saved?
___2n − 15___ What equals the total amount? __$n + (2n − 15) = 120$__
Simplify: ___$3n − 15 = 120$___ Solve.

How much has George saved? __$45__

How much has Cindy saved? __$75__

SHOW YOUR WORK

Solve each problem.

1. Nate and Laura picked apples. Laura picked $\frac{1}{2}$ as many as Nate picked. Together they picked 90 apples. How many did each of them pick?

    Let *n* stand for the number Nate picked.

    Equation: _____
    How many apples did Nate pick? _____
    How many apples did Laura pick? _____

2. Jordan travels $\frac{3}{4}$ of a mile longer to school each day than Harrison does. Combined, they travel $5\frac{1}{4}$ miles to school. How far does each travel?

    Let *n* stand for the distance Jordan travels.

    Equation: _____
    How far does Jordan travel? _____
    How far does Harrison travel? _____

3. Two jackets have a combined cost of $98. Jacket A costs $12 less than Jacket B. How much does each jacket cost?

    Let *n* stand for the cost of Jacket A.

    Equation: _____
    Jacket A costs _____
    Jacket B costs _____.

1.

2.

3.

Lesson 6.6 Dependent and Independent Variables

Sometimes, word problems contain dependent and independent variables. The **dependent variable** in a problem is the value that is affected by the other values in the problem. The **independent variable** is the value that affects the outcome of the dependent variable.

If a car has to travel 200 miles, the speed (*s*) the car is driving is the independent variable and the time (*t*) it takes to make the trip is the dependent variable. This can be represented by the formula, $200 = s \times t$, and can be solved by creating a table.

Dependent Variable	Time	5 hours	4 hours	$3\frac{1}{3}$ hours
Independent Variable	Speed	40 miles/hr.	50 miles/hr.	60 miles/hr.

Use tables to identify the variables and find possible solutions to the problems.

1. Maria has to buy apples at the grocery store. Apples cost $1.25 per pound. How much will Maria spend on apples?

   What equation will you use? _____

Dependent Variable				
Independent Variable				

2. When a tree is planted, it is 6 feet tall. Each year, it grows by 2 feet. How tall will it get over time?

   What equation will you use? _____

_____ Variable	Height			
_____ Variable	Time	3 years	6 years	9 years

3. The graph shows the amount of water in a pool as it is constantly filling over time.

   Write an equation that can be used to find the number of gallons, *y*, after *x* minutes.

   _____

   How long will it take for 40 gallons of water to fill the pool?

   _____

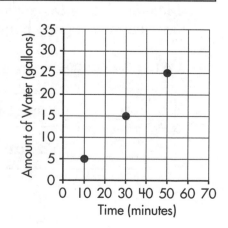

Check What You Learned

Expressions and Equations

Create expressions equivalent to the ones below.

1. $4(a + b)$ _____

2. $3(9a + 8b)$ _____

3. $9(x + 2y)$ _____

4. $2(9x + 3^2)$ _____

5. $5^3(2 + 4c)$ _____

6. $\frac{x + x}{3}$ _____

7. $4^2(12 + 5c)$ _____

8. $17(14r + 3^3) - 7r$ _____

Use the distributive property and greatest common factor to factor each expression.

9. $6n + 72$ _____

10. $3t + 21s$ _____

11. $7b - 42a$ _____

Use the table to identify the variables and find possible solutions to the problems.

12. Students have been assigned to read a book that is 150 pages. Every student reads at a different speed. Depending on reading speed, how many days will it take different students to read the assigned book?

Write the equation: _____

_____ **Variable**	Time (Days)			
_____ **Variable**	Reading Speed per Day	15 pages	20 pages	30 pages

Check What You Learned

Expressions and Equations

Solve the problem. Write each answer in simplest form.

13. Drew spent $38.97 on $3\frac{1}{4}$ pounds of shrimp. How much does a pound of shrimp cost?

A pound of shrimp costs _____.

Solve each problem.

14. Samantha can run 5 miles per hour while Steve can run 4 miles per hour. If they both run for 2.5 hours, how much farther will Samantha run?

Let d represent the distance.
Equation: _____
Another way of writing this is: _____
Samantha will run _____ miles farther.

15. Walker is reading a book that is 792 pages. He reads 15 pages a day during the week, and 25 pages a day during the weekend. After 5 weeks of reading, how many pages does Walker still have left to read before he finishes the book?

Let r represent the pages left to read.
Equation: _____
Walker has _____ pages left to read.

16. The graph shows the distance a freight train is constantly traveling over time.

Write an equation that can be used to find the number of miles traveled, y, in x minutes.

_____

How long will it take for the train to travel 24 miles?

_____

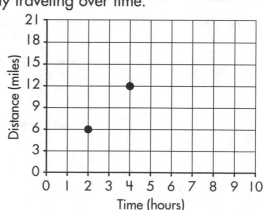

NAME _____

Check What You Know

Equations and Inequalities

Solve each equation. Write *null* if the equation has no solution. Write *all* if all numbers solve the equation. Write fractions in simplest form.

	a	**b**
1.	$15 + n = 2n$ _____	$7 - p = 3p + 5$ _____
2.	$6y + 2 = 4y$ _____	$0.6x = 2.2x - 4$ _____
3.	$\frac{2r}{3} = 10 - r$ _____	$3(m + 2) = 21$ _____
4.	$14 = 2(n - 3) + 6$ _____	$5(b + 4) = 5(b + 6) - 10$ _____
5.	$4(z - 1) = 3(z + 2)$ _____	$7(a + 3) = 7a + 11$ _____

Write $\leq$ or $\geq$ on the line to complete the inequality.

6. Carmen will make at least $30 doing chores. Carmen's earnings will be _____ $30.

7. To lose weight, Brad wants to consume no more than 2,000 calories a day. Brad wants his daily consumption to be _____ 2,000 calories.

Solve each inequality and graph its solution.

8 $h \div 6 < -12$

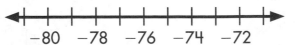

9. $-10a > -70$

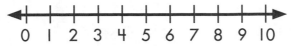

Check What You Know

Equations and Inequalities

Write an inequality for each problem. Use *n* as the variable. Then, solve the inequality. Include the proper inequality symbol in the solution.

10. An auto mechanic estimates that the cost to repair Brett's car will be no more than $200. The parts will cost $49.23. What is the estimated cost for the labor?

Inequality: _____ Solution: _____

11. Tawana has $325.54 in her checking account. She must keep a balance of at least $300 to avoid a fee. She plans to write a check to pay her credit card bill of $125.43. How much money must Tawana deposit in her account to maintain at least the minimum balance?

Inequality: _____ Solution: _____

Solve the inequalities and represent the possible values of the variable on a number line.

12. $6 > z - 2$

13. $g + 7 < -12$

14. $d - 5 < 7$

15. $15 > k + 2$

16. $1 + x > -16$

17. $y + 8 < -9$

18. $8 \leq 8 + r$

19. $w + 8 \geq 11$

Lesson 7.1 Equations with Variables on Each Side

Sometimes a variable appears on both sides of an equation. When this happens, use the properties of equality to rewrite the equation with the variable on the one side. Then, solve.

$4 + 3x = 5x$

$4 + 3x - 3x = 5x - 3x$ Subtraction Property

$4 = 2x$ Simplify

$\frac{4}{2} = \frac{2x}{2}$ Division Property

$2 = x$ Solution

$2n = -4n - 3$

$2n + 4n = -4n - 3 + 4n$ Addition Property

$6n = -3$ Simplify

$\frac{6n}{6} = \frac{-3}{6}$ Division Property

$n = \frac{-1}{2}$ Solution

Solve each equation. Write fractions in simplest form.

	a	b
1.	$8b + 2 = 10b$ _____	$15 + c = 2c - 5$ _____
2.	$7t + 2t = t - 6$ _____	$28 + p = 15p$ _____
3.	$30x + 3 = 10 - 5x$ _____	$0.23n = 2.73n - 5$ _____
4.	$6a + 9 = 3a$ _____	$1.4x - 8 = x + 12$ _____
5.	$-2d = 4d - 42$ _____	$\frac{8g}{4} = g + 9$ _____
6.	$4m + 24 = 36 + m$ _____	$2r = 4r - 14.2$ _____

Write an equation for each statement, using x for the variable. Then, solve the equation.

7. Three times a number plus 5 equals 10 more than the same number.

Equation: _____   Solution: _____

8. Six more than half of a number equals the same number times 2.

Equation: _____   Solution: _____

Lesson 7.2 Equations with Grouping Symbols

To solve equations with grouping symbols, such as parentheses, first use the distributive property to remove the parentheses. Then, solve.

Solve: $3(2 + n) = 10 + 2n$

$(3 \times 2) + (3 \times n) = 10 + 2n$ Distributive Property

$6 + 3n = 10 + 2n$ Simplify

$6 + 3n - 2n = 10 + 2n - 2n$ Subtraction Property

$6 + n = 10$ Simplify

$6 + n - 6 = 10 - 6$ Subtraction Property

$n = 4$ Solution

Some equations have no solutions. The symbol $\varnothing$ means **null**, or no solution. Some equations have an infinite number of solutions, or true for all solutions.

$2 + a = 4 + a$

$2 + a - a = 4 + a - a$

$2 = 4$

This equation is never true. Therefore, the solution is $\varnothing$ (null).

$10b - 5 = 2(5b - 2) - 1$

$10b - 5 = 10b - 4 - 1$

$10b - 5 = 10b - 5$

$10b = 10b$ after adding 5 to each side

$b = b$ after dividing each side by 10

This equation is always true. Therefore, the solution is true for all numbers.

Solve the equations. Write *null* or *all* where appropriate. Show fractions in simplest form.

	a	b
1.	$5(y + 2) = 20$ _____	$16 = 4(n - 5) + 4$ _____
2.	$2(x - 4) = 2x - 8$ _____	$7p + 9 = 4(p - 3)$ _____
3.	$6(k + 3) = 2(4k + 5)$ _____	$3(2m + 4) = 6m + 15$ _____
4.	$30 - 2x = 2(3x + 3)$ _____	$2(4w + 7) = 3(6 + 2w)$ _____
5.	$6(2 + 3z) = 3(4 + 6z)$ _____	$25 = 6(c + 7) - 14$ _____
6.	$4g + 9 = 2(g - 6) + 2g$ _____	$3(3h + h) = 2(h + 5)$ _____

Lesson 7.3 Inequalities

Recall that the = symbol means *equal to*. This symbol indicates an equation, or equality. An **inequality** states that values are not equal. The symbols > and < indicate inequality. Sometimes the values in an inequality might also be equal. For example, a tank holds 15 gallons of gas. How much gas is in the tank? You don't know without measuring. However, you do know that the amount must be less than or equal to 15 gallons: Gas in tank ≤ 15 gallons.

Symbol	Meaning
>	greater than
<	less than
≥	greater than or equal to
≤	less than or equal to

Sometimes you can use the text in an item to determine when to use the less than or equal to or greater than or equal to symbols. Terms such as "no more than" or "at most" indicate that ≤ should be used. Terms such as "at least" indicate that ≥ should be used.

Tim wants to run no more than 5 miles can be represented by $x ≤ 5$ miles.

Shauna wants to work at least 4 hours can be represented by $x ≥ 4$ hours.

Write ≥ or ≤ on the line to complete the inequality.

1. In 1 year, Lana wants to save at least $500. Lana wants her savings to be _____ $500.

2. Jordan takes $20 to the mall. Using cash only, Jordan will spend _____ $20.

3. Luis wants to bike at least 20 miles today. Luis wants to bike _____ 20 miles.

4. Maria wants her plant to grow to at most 12 inches tall. Maria wants her plant to grow _____ 12 inches tall.

Write an inequality that describes the situation.

5. Trudi plans to study no more than 2 hours. _____

6. There are at least 32 students that want to go to the museum. _____

NAME _____

Lesson 7.4 Solving Inequalities by Adding or Subtracting

The addition and subtraction properties also apply to inequalities. You can add or subtract the same number from both sides of an inequality without affecting the inequality.

Solve: $n + 4 < 9$ $n + 4 - 4 < 9 - 4$ $n < 5$

The solution is that n can be any value less than 5.

If you swap the left side and right side of an inequality, you must reverse the direction of the inequality. The direction is the way the arrow points.

$n < 5$	$x - 6 > 3$	$p \leq 9$	$k - 7 \geq 6$
$5 > n$	$3 < x - 6$	$9 \geq p$	$6 \leq k - 7$
$<$ becomes $>$	$>$ becomes $<$	$\leq$ becomes $\geq$	$\geq$ becomes $\leq$

When the solution includes an arrow pointing in the positive or negative direction, the solution includes all of the numbers in that direction. So, there are an infinite number of values for the solution.

Solve the inequalities and represent the possible values of the variable on a number line.

1. $x + 2 < 4$

2. $t - 3 > 2$

3. $1 < 2 + k$

4. $3 > 2 + k$

Write an inequality for each problem. Use n as the variable. Then, solve the inequality. Include the proper inequality symbol in the solution.

5. Jermaine has $25. He wants to buy a pair of gloves that costs $16.50. He also wants to buy a sandwich. How much can Jermaine spend on the sandwich?

   Inequality: _____   Solution: _____

6. Sharon has jogged 1.25 miles. Her goal is to jog more than 3.5 miles. How much more must she jog to accomplish her goal?

   Inequality: _____   Solution: _____

Lesson 7.5 Solving Inequalities by Multiplying or Dividing

Multiplication and division properties also apply to inequalities. You can multiply or divide both sides of an inequality by the same positive number without affecting the inequality. But if you multiply or divide both sides by a negative number, you must reverse the direction of the inequality.

Solve: $4x > 12$	Solve: $\frac{n}{2} \le 8$	Solve: $-3p < 6$
$\frac{4x}{4} > \frac{12}{4}$	$\frac{n}{2} \times 2 \le 8 \times 2$	$\frac{-3p}{-3} > \frac{6}{-3}$ reverse the
$x > 3$	$n \le 16$	$p > -2$ inequality

Remember to reverse the direction of the inequality if you swap the left and the right sides.

Solve each inequality. Show the solution on a number line.

1. $12 \le 4n$ _____

2. $-7h < 28$ _____

3. $9 \le \frac{n}{3}$ _____

4. $4 > -4n$ _____

Write an inequality for each problem. Use n as the variable. Then, solve the inequality. Include the proper inequality symbol in the solution.

5. Kevin has $26 and wants to rent a bicycle. The bicycle rents for $6.25 per hour. How many hours can Kevin ride without owing more money than he has?

Inequality: _____ Solution: _____

6. Shia wants to save the same amount each month. In 4 months, she wants savings of at least $200. How much money must Shia save each month to achieve her goal?

Inequality: _____ Solution: _____

Lesson 7.6 Solving Multi-Step Inequalities

Some problems with inequalities require more than one step to solve. Use the properties of equality to solve the inequality. Remember to reverse the direction of the inequality if you multiply or divide by a negative number or if you swap the sides of the inequality.

$4n + 6 < 18$		$6 - 2n \geq 24$	
$4n + 6 - 6 < 18 - 6$	Subtraction Property	$6 - 2n - 6 \geq 24 - 6$	Subtraction Property
$4n < 12$	Simplify	$-2n \geq 18$	Simplify
$\frac{4n}{4} < \frac{12}{4}$	Division Property	$\frac{-2n}{-2} \leq \frac{18}{-2}$	Reverse direction
$n < 3$	Solution	$n \leq -9$	Solution

Solve each inequality. Show the solution on a number line.

1. $-6x + 4 > 40$ _____

2. $\frac{3z}{5} \geq 9$ _____

3. $\frac{4m}{-3} \geq 12$ _____

4. $5y - 0.25 < 6$ _____

Write an inequality for each problem. Use n as the variable. Then, solve the inequality.

5. Josh wants to download music online. He must buy a membership for $14. Then, he can download songs for 99 cents each. Josh has $20. How many songs can Josh buy without spending more money than he has?

    Inequality: _____ Solution: _____

6. Kendra makes $8 per hour mowing lawns in the summer. Gas for the mower costs $16 and will last all summer. How many hours must Kendra mow to earn at least $200?

    Inequality: _____ Solution: _____

Lesson 7.7 Linear Equations in One Variable

When solving a linear equation in one variable, there are three possible results.

You may solve the equation for **one** specific value of the variable. There may be **infinitely many** solutions to a linear equation or there may be **no** solutions to a linear equation.

For a linear equation with one solution, only one value will satisfy the equation.

$$3x + 5 = 11 + x$$
$$2x = 6$$
$$x = 3$$

For a linear equation with no solution, the given solution is not true.

$$2t + 3 = 2(t + 2)$$
$$2t + 3 = 2t + 4$$
$$3 = 4$$

For a linear equation with infinitely many solutions, any value for the variable will satisfy the equation.

$$4n + 6 = 2(2n + 3)$$
$$4n + 6 = 4n + 6$$
$$4n = 4n$$
$$n = n$$

Solve each equation. Indicate if an equation has *no solution* or *infinitely many solutions*.

	a	**b**
1.	$2x + 4 = 9 + x$ _____	$4t + 3 = 4(t + 1)$ _____
2.	$5a + 5 = 5(a + 1)$ _____	$6z + z = 5z + 10$ _____
3.	$b + 3b - 10 = 2(2b - 5)$ _____	$2c - c = 3c - 5$ _____
4.	$y + 5y - 6 = 3(2y - 2)$ _____	$12n + 7 = 4n + 8n + 6$ _____
5.	$-4t - 11 = \frac{4t}{2} + 7$ _____	$12d(3 - 2) = 24$ _____
6.	$-4z + 6 = 4(-z + 2)$ _____	$4x = x + 10.5$ _____

Check What You Learned

Equations and Inequalities

Solve each equation. Write *null* if the equation has no solution. Write *all* if all numbers solve the equation. Write fractions in simplest form.

	a	**b**
1.	$33 + a = 12a$ _____	$-6n + 2 = 4n - 5$ _____
2.	$2.4b - 7 = b + 15.4$ _____	$\frac{4m}{6} = m + 3$ _____
3.	$4p + \frac{1}{4} = 6p$ _____	$24 - c = 2(3 + 4c)$ _____
4.	$3(5 - 2y) = 4(y + 2)$ _____	$5(2x + 3) = 3(x + 2) + 7x + 9$ _____
5.	$4(3k + 6) = 12(5 + k)$ _____	$3(2n + 4) = 2n + 56$ _____

Write $\leq$ or $\geq$ on the line to complete the inequality.

6. A polling company needs at least 250 responses for its survey to be valid. The number of responses must be _____ 250.

7. If Rima can sign up 10 people or more to attend a concert, everyone will get a discount on the ticket price. Rima needs a group that is _____ 10.

Solve the inequality and represent the possible values of the variable on a number line.

8. $8 > z - 2$

9. Explain how many solutions there are to $3x + 2 \geq 17$.

_____

_____

CHAPTER 7 POSTTEST

Check What You Learned

Equations and Inequalities

Solve each inequality. Write the solution with the variable on the left side.

	a	**b**	**c**

10. $b - 9 < 18$ _____ $11 + k > 24$ _____ $23 < 7 + p$ _____

11. $-3 \geq n - 8$ _____ $\frac{y}{3} < 12$ _____ $10x \geq 35$ _____

12. $-3a > -21$ _____ $\frac{c}{-2} \geq 6$ _____ $88 \leq 4t$ _____

13. $6 > -2d$ _____ $-8 < \frac{g}{-2}$ _____ $4y + 8 < 20$ _____

14. $12 \leq 7x - 2$ _____ $\frac{3n}{4} \geq 12$ _____ $45 > 11k + 1$ _____

15. $2.5 < 2 + 5p$ _____ $6\% + 4a \leq 90\%$ _____ $21 < 9 - 6b$ _____

Write an inequality for each problem. Use n as the variable. Then, solve the inequality. Include the proper inequality symbol in the solution.

16. Hajime wants to advertise the class carwash in the local newspaper. He can spend no more than $35 on the advertisement. The newspaper charges 85 cents per word. How many words can Hajime have in the ad?

Inequality: _____ Solution: _____

17. Silvia has a bucket that holds 4.5 quarts of liquid. She put 1.25 quarts of water in the bucket. How much more water can she add without exceeding the amount the bucket can hold?

Inequality: _____ Solution: _____

Check What You Know

Functions and Graphing

Complete the function table for each function. Then, graph the function.

a

1. $y = x - 4$

x	y

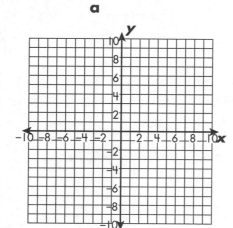

$y = 3x + 1$

x	y

b

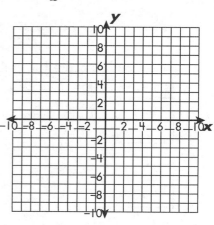

Graph the solution to each inequality.

2. $y > x - 2$

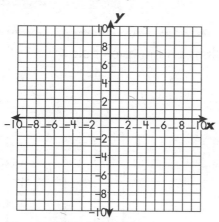

$y < 3x + 2$

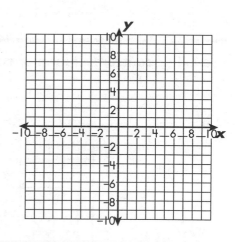

Answer each question.

3. If you know that the direct variation equation is $y = 5x$ and $y = 15$, what is x? _____

4. Using the same equation, what is y if $x = 8$? _____

5. Nicole ran 2 miles in 15 minutes. Express her rate of speed as a direct variation equation, using d for distance and t for time (in minutes). _____

6. At that rate, how long would it take her to run 6 miles? _____

NAME _____

Check What You Know

Functions and Graphing

Write a linear equation from the information given below.

7. The slope is 3 and the line passes through point (5, 17). _____

8. The line passes through points (4, 5) and (6, 9). _____

9. The function table for the line is shown below.

x	y
−2	3
−1	4
0	5
1	6
2	7
3	8

_____

10. The graph for the line is shown at right.

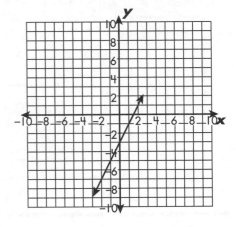

_____

Use the slope-intercept form of equations to draw lines on the grids below.

a

b

11.

$y = 3x + 2$

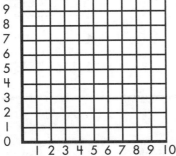

$y = -2x + 8$

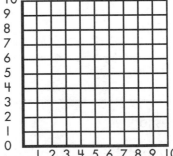

Find the constant of proportionality for each set of values.

12.

x	1.5	3	4.5	12
y	1	2	3	8

x	2	4	7	9
y	0.4	0.8	1.4	1.8

$k =$ _____

$k =$ _____

Lesson 8.1 Functions and Function Tables

A **function** is a rule for how two variables relate. For each value of x (the domain), there is only one value of y (the range). For example, if $y = x + 6$, whatever x is, y must be greater than x by the number 6.

A **function table** shows the values for each pair of variables as the result of the particular function. A function table for the equation $y = x + 6$ is shown here.

x	y
-1	5
0	6
1	7
2	8
3	9
4	10

Complete each function table for the given functions.

	a	**b**	**c**

1.

a $y = x - 3$

x	y
0	
1	
2	
3	
4	
5	

b $y = 4x + 2$

x	y
-2	
-1	
0	
1	
2	
3	

c $y = 3x - 1$

x	y
-3	
-2	
-1	
0	
1	
2	

2.

a $y = \frac{x}{2}$

x	y
-2	
0	
2	
4	
6	
8	

b $y = \frac{x}{4} + 2$

x	y
-8	
-4	
0	
4	
8	
12	

c $y = \frac{x}{3} - 1$

x	y
-9	
-6	
-3	
0	
3	
6	

3.

a $y = x^2 + 5$

x	y
0	
1	
2	
3	
4	
5	

b $y = 2x^2 - 1$

x	y
0	
1	
2	
3	
4	
5	

c $y = (x + 1) \div 2$

x	y
-5	
-3	
-1	
1	
3	
5	

Lesson 8.2 Graphing Linear Equations

A **linear equation** is an equation that creates a straight line when graphed on a coordinate plane. To graph a linear equation, create a function table with at least 3 ordered pairs. Then, plot these ordered pairs on a coordinate plane. Draw a line through the points. Some points for this linear equation are in the table to the right:

$$y = \frac{x}{2} + 1$$

These points are plotted on the line graph at the right.

x	y
-2	0
0	1
2	2
4	3

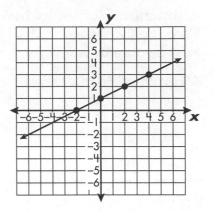

Complete the function table for each function. Then, graph the function.

a **b**

1. $y = x + 3$ $y = 4x - 1$

x	y

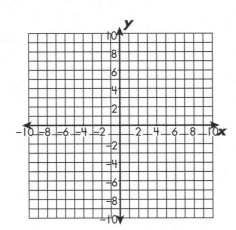

x	y

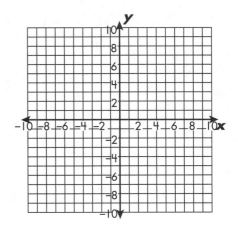

2. $y = \frac{x}{2} - 1$ $y = \frac{x}{3} - 1$

x	y

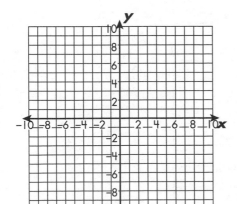

x	y

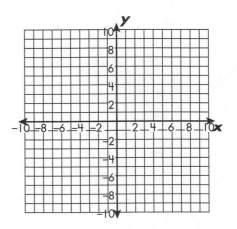

Lesson 8.3 Slope and y-Intercept

Every straight line can be represented by the equation $y = mx + b$, where m is the slope of the line and b is the y-intercept.

The **slope** of a line is its steepness or slant. It is calculated as follows:

$$m = \frac{\text{change in } y\text{-value}}{\text{change in } x\text{-value}} \qquad = \frac{y_2 - y_1}{x_2 - x_1}$$

where (x_1, y_1) and (x_2, y_2) are two different points on the line.

The **y-intercept** is the value of y at the point where the line crosses the x-axis (that is, where $x = 0$).

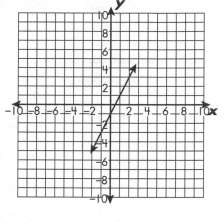

In the graph to the right, the slope (m) for the line $= \frac{(3 - 1)}{(2 - 1)} = 2$.

The line intersects the y-axis at the point $(0, -1)$, so -1 is the y-intercept.

Find the slope and y-intercept for each line.

<table>
<tr><td align="center">**a**</td><td align="center">**b**</td><td align="center">**c**</td></tr>
</table>

1.

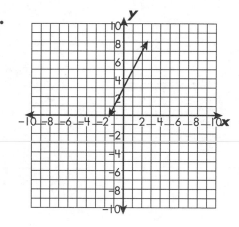 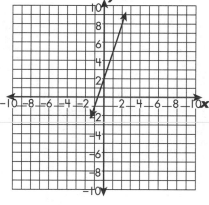 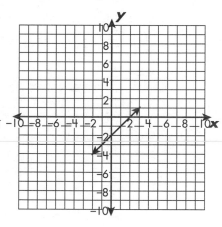

slope _____   slope _____   slope _____

y-intercept _____   y-intercept _____   y-intercept _____

2. The total cost to produce a shipment of shoes is the fixed cost (the costs that you have even if you produce no shoes, such as equipment) plus the variable cost (the costs that increase as you produce more shoes, such as materials).

a. If you were to graph these costs, which would be the y-intercept? _____

b. Which would be the slope? _____

Lesson 8.4 Slope and Similar Triangles

The rate of change, or slope, of a line can be tested for constancy by using similar triangles.

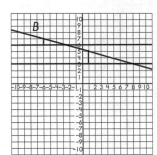

To test if the slope of the line B is constant, draw a set of parallel lines that intersect the line.

Then, draw a line segment from each of the parallel lines to line B to create a set of right triangles.

Find the length of the legs for each set of triangles. 3 & 1 and 6 & 2

Test the leg lengths for proportionality. $\frac{3}{1} = \frac{6}{2}$

$3 \times 2 = 6$ and $6 \times 1 = 6$

These leg lengths are proportional, so the line has a constant slope.

Use similar right triangles to prove that each line has a constant slope.

a   **b**

1.

Triangle 1 Legs:

_____ & _____

Triangle 2 Legs:

_____ & _____

Proportionality Test:

___ = ___

Triangle 1 Legs:

_____ & _____

Triangle 2 Legs:

_____ & _____

Proportionality Test:

___ = ___

2.

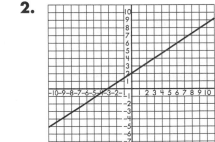

Triangle 1 Legs:

_____ & _____

Triangle 2 Legs:

_____ & _____

Proportionality Test:

___ = ___

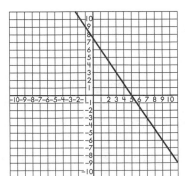

Triangle 1 Legs:

_____ & _____

Triangle 2 Legs:

_____ & _____

Proportionality Test:

___ = ___

Lesson 8.5   Rate of Change

Rate of change is the speed at which a variable changes over a specific amount of time. The slope of a line shows the rate of change of one variable with respect to another variable.

The graph to the right shows that as x increases by 1, y increases by 2, so the rate of change (or slope) is 2.

If you know that y and x are directly proportional to each other, you can write an equation that relates the two quantities. This is called a **direct variation** equation, since y is said to **vary directly** with x. This equation has the form $y = kx$, where $k \neq 0$. k is called the **constant of variation** or the **constant of proportionality**. For the line in the graph, the direct variation equation is $y = 2x$.

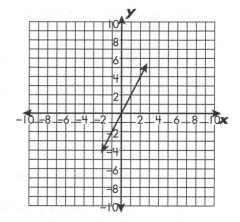

Answer each question.

1. If you know that the direct variation equation is $y = 3x$ and $y = 12$, what is x? _____

2. Using the same equation, what is y if $x = 5$? _____

3. A train travels 400 km in 2 hours.

    a. What is the rate? _____

    b. Write a direct variation equation that expresses this relationship,

    using d for distance and t for time (in hours). _____

    c. How many hours would it take the train to travel 300 km? It would take _____ hours.

Find the slope, or rate of change for each situation. Be sure to show your work.

4. Students are buying tickets for the fall dance. The student council keeps track of how many tickets they sell in one week.

	Monday	Tuesday	Wednesday	Thursday	Friday
Number of Tickets Sold	10	15	23	28	32
Amount Earned ($)	50	75	115	140	160

   If the data is graphed and passes through (0, 0) and (1, 5), what is the constant of proportionality of the relationship between number of tickets sold and amount earned?

   _____

Lesson 8.6 Writing Linear Equations

You can write a linear equation if you know the slope and one point on the line:

1. In the equation $y = mx + b$, replace m with the given slope and x and y with the coordinates of the given point.

2. Solve the equation for the y-intercept (b).

3. Write the equation, replacing m with the slope and b with the y-intercept.

You can also write a linear equation if you know two points on the line:

1. Use the formula $\frac{y_2 - y_1}{x_2 - x_1}$ to calculate m.

2. Choose either of the two points to use in place of x and y in the equation $y = mx + b$. Replace m with the slope you calculated.

3. Solve the equation for the y-intercept (b).

4. Write the equation, replacing m with the slope and b with the y-intercept.

Write a linear equation from the information given below.

1. The slope is 2 and the line passes through point (6, 13). _____

2. The slope is 1 and the line passes through point (−4, −6). _____

3. The line passes through points (2, 7) and (4, 8). _____

4. The line passes through points (0, 5) and (−2, 1). _____

5. The function table for the line is given below. **6.** The graph for the line is shown below.

x	y
0	−7
2	−5
5	−2
7	0
10	3
15	8

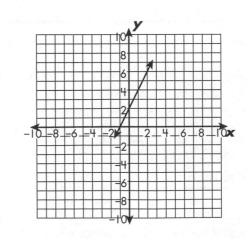

_____   _____

Lesson 8.7 Graphing Polygons: Rectangles

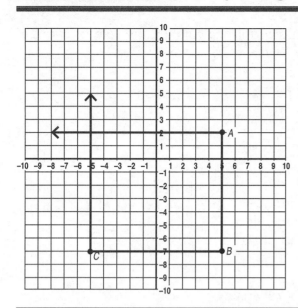

Coordinate planes can help you solve problems with polygons, such as rectangles.

If points A (5, 2), B (5, −7), and C (−5, −7) are vertices of a rectangle, where does vertex D fall?

Connect the vertices and then draw lines straight from points A and C to find where vertex D will fall.

Point D occurs at point (−5, 2).

Use the coordinate grids to find the missing vertex of each polygon.

1. a rectangle with points at (0, 2), (−6, 2), and (−6, 4)

   The missing point is at _____.

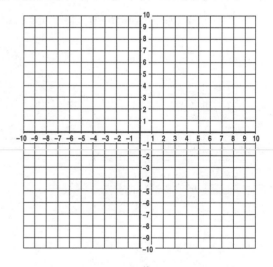

2. a rectangle with points at (3, −4), (3, 5), and (−2, 5)

   The missing point is at _____.

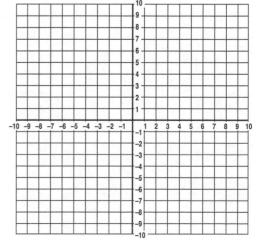

Lesson 8.8 Constructing Function Models

Function models can be constructed by observing points on a graph, calculating the rate of change (or slope), and plugging known values into the equation, $y = mx + b$.

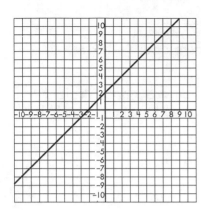

Step 1: Find and name two points on the line.

$(4, 6)$ and $(2, 4)$

Step 2: Calculate the rate of change.

$m = \frac{4 - 6}{2 - 4} = \frac{-2}{-2} = 1$

Step 3: Use the found points and calculated slope to find the initial value of the output if it cannot be determined based on the graph.

Based on the graph, the initial value of the output variable is 2.

Step 4: Write the formula for all values of x and y using the equation.

$y = (1)x + 2$
$y = x + 2$

Use the graphs to write function models, or equations, in the form of $y = mx + b$.

a

b

1.

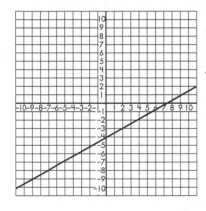

Function Model:

_____

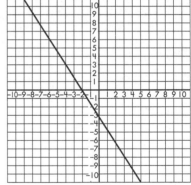

Function Model:

_____

2.

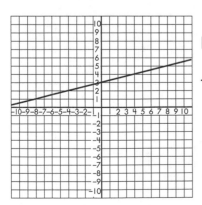

Function Model:

_____

Function Model:

_____

Lesson 8.9 Analyzing Function Graphs

Models of real-life situations can be drawn on non-specific graphs—or ones without titles or labeled x and y axes—in order to see the relationship between two variables that are being examined along different points.

Situation:

Mike rides a bike to Sam's house. When he arrives, he and Sam wait for Sam's mom who then drives them to the bus stop. Sam and Mike wait for the bus, and then get on the bus, which then takes them to school.

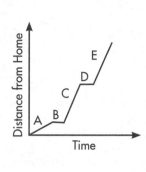

Relationships:

Mike travels at a constant rate to Sam's house (A).

Mike and Sam do not travel while they wait for Sam's mom to drive them to the bus stop (B).

Sam's mom takes Mike and Sam to the bus stop (C).

Mike and Sam do not travel while they are waiting at the bus stop (D).

Mike and Sam appear to travel at the same constant rate both in the car and on the bus (E).

Use the situation and graph to describe 3 relationships that exist in each function.

1. Situation:
An amusement park is open from April to November each year. The graph shows the number of visitors it receives.

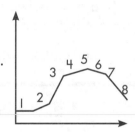

Relationships:

_____
_____
_____
_____
_____

2. Situation:
Grace is studying words for a spelling bee. She has 4 weeks to learn as many as she can.

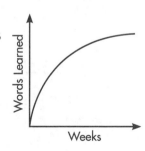

Relationships:

_____
_____
_____
_____
_____

3. Situation:
A family is taking a 500 mile trip to visit family.

Relationships:

_____
_____
_____
_____
_____

Lesson 8.10 Graphing Linear Inequalities

The slope-intercept form of a linear function, $y = mx + b$, can be used to create a graph of that function. $y = 2x - 7$

Step 1: Mark the point where the line will cross the y-axis $(b = -7)$.

Step 2: From the point which crosses the y-axis, use the slope (m) to find other points on both sides. Remember that slope is found by $\frac{change\ in\ y}{change\ in\ x}$.

Step 3: Draw a line that goes directly through the points found.

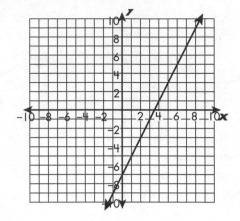

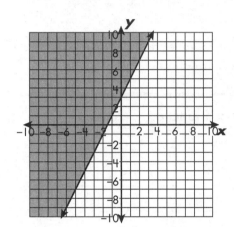

A linear inequality is an inequality that has the form $y \geq mx + b$, $y \leq mx + b$, $y > mx + b$, or $y < mx + b$.

To graph a linear inequality, first graph the line for $y = mx + b$. For inequalities of the form $y \geq mx + b$, shade the area above the line. For inequalities of the form $y \leq mx + b$, shade the area below the line. For inequalities of the form $y > mx + b$ or $y < mx + b$, use a dashed line, rather than a solid line, to indicate that the line itself is not part of the inequality.

The graph to the right shows the inequality $y \geq 2x + 3$.

1. Graph the solution to $y < x - 3$.

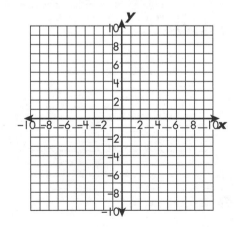

2. Graph the linear equation $y = \frac{1}{6}x$

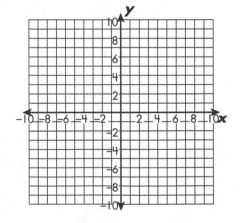

Lesson 8.11 Defining Functions

A function is a relationship between two variables which results in only one output value for each input value. If one input has more than one output, then a function does not exist.

input	output
3	−2
4	−3
5	−1

This table represents a function because for every input variable, there is one and only one output variable.

input	output
3	10, 20
6	15

This table does not represent a function because one of the input variables has more than one output variable.

In a function, each value of **x** relates to only one value of **y**. For example, if $y = x + 6$, whatever x is, y must be greater than x by the number 6.

A **function table** shows the values for each pair of variables as the result of the particular function.

Decide if each table represents a function by stating *yes* or *no*.

a

input	output
−9	d
−5	c
1	b
6	a

b

input	output
2	4
4	6
6	8

c

input	output
−4	0
−1	6, −6
0	4

1.

_____   _____   _____

Complete each function table for the given function.

2.

x	y
−10	−4
−2	4
0	
3	
5	
8	

x	y
0	−2
1	−1
3	
5	
8	
10	

x	y
0	−7
2	−5
5	
7	
10	
15	

Lesson 8.12 Functions and Linear Relationships

Data in tables can be used to create equations. If the table of values represents a function, a linear relationship in the form of $y = mx + b$ exists.

x	y
99	9
72	6
54	4
27	1

Step 1: Find the rate of change by calculating the slope, or rate of change, between the two variables. $\frac{y_2 - y_1}{x_2 - x_1}$

Step 2: Substitute known values of x and y with the slope into the formula $y = mx + b$.

Step 3: Use the found values in the linear function to complete the table.

$\frac{9-1}{99-27} = \frac{8}{72} = \frac{1}{9}$

$9 = \left(\frac{1}{9}\right)(99) + b$
$9 = \left(\frac{1}{9}\right)(99) + b$
$9 - 11 = 11 + b - 11$
$-2 = b$

$y = \left(\frac{1}{9}\right)(72) - 2$
$y = 8 - 2 = 6$

Not all function tables represent a linear relationship. If the rate of change, or slope, is not constant, then the function does not represent a linear relationship.

Test the rate of change by using the slope formula across multiple points on the table.

Linear Relationship

x	y	Rate
1	217	217
2	434	
3	651	217
4	868	

Non linear Relationship

x	y	Rate
−1	0	−5
0	−5	
1	−8	−1
2	−9	

Find the relationship for each function table and then complete the table.

a

1.

x	y
12	
24	
84	7
120	10

Function: _____

b

x	y
2	
4	7
5	
11	14

Function: _____

Find the rate of change, or slope, for points on the function table and decide if it represents a *linear* or *nonlinear* relationship.

2.

x	y	Rate
−10	−10	
−5	−7	
0	−4	
5	−1	

Relationship:

_____

x	y	Rate
−3	−15	
1	−8	
5	−1	
9	6	

Relationship:

_____

NAME _____

Lesson 8.13 Constructing Function Models

Function models, or equations, can be constructed by using known values of input (x) and output (y) variables, the rate of change (m), and the initial value of the output variable (b) in the format, $y = mx + b$.

Step 1: Calculate the rate of change. $\qquad \frac{12 - 5}{5 - 2} = \frac{7}{3}$

Step 2: Substitute known values of x and y into the slope-intercept form of the equation.

$$y = mx + b$$
$$(2) = \left(\frac{7}{3}\right)(2) + b$$

Step 3: Solve to find the initial value of the output variable (b).

$$2 = \frac{14}{3} + b$$
$$b = 2 - \frac{14}{3} = -\frac{8}{3}$$

Step 4: Write the equation using the found values of m and b.

$$y = \frac{7}{3}x + \left(-\frac{8}{3}\right) \text{ or } \frac{7}{3}x - \frac{8}{3}$$

Construct a function model, or equation, for each table below.

a

1.

input	output
1	3
2	6
3	9

Function Model: _____

b

input	output
3	1
6	2
9	3

Function Model: _____

c

input	output
1	6
3	18
5	30

Function Model: _____

2.

input	output
2	2
3	4
4	6

Function Model: _____

input	output
2	1
4	4
6	7

Function Model: _____

input	output
12	4
16	8
20	12

Function Model: _____

3.

input	output
2	−1
4	1
6	3

Function Model: _____

input	output
1	3
2	7
3	11

Function Model: _____

input	output
0	6
1	8
3	12

Function Model: _____

Lesson 8.14   Comparing Functions

Functions that are represented in different ways can be compared by their rate of change or by specific values at a certain point. The functions do not have to be in the same format in order to compare them.

Which function has a greater rate of change?

$y = -\frac{16}{5}x + 6$ or

x	0	1	2
y	1	−3	−7

Rate of change for table $= \frac{-7 - 1}{2 - 0} = -\frac{8}{2} = -4$

Rate of change is judged by larger absolute value, therefore, the rate of change for the function represented in the table is larger than the rate of change shown by the equation.

Compare the rate of change for the equations and tables shown below and decide which has a greater rate of change by writing *equation* or *table*.

a

1. $y = 2x + 6$ or

x	0	1	2
y	10	16	26

_____

2. $y = 7x + 4$ or

x	0	1	2
y	8	10	12

_____

3. $y = 5x + 2$ or

x	0	1	2
y	3	10	17

_____

4. $y = 7x + 4$ or

x	0	1	2
y	1	−3	−7

_____

b

$y = 4x + 7$ or

x	0	1	2
y	9	12	15

_____

$y = 3x + 4$ or

x	0	1	2
y	7	12	17

_____

$y = \frac{3}{2}x - 2$ or

x	0	1	2
y	−2	−1	0

_____

$y = \frac{3}{2}x + 2$ or

x	0	1	2
y	1	$\frac{7}{3}$	$\frac{11}{23}$

_____

Check What You Learned

Functions and Graphing

Complete the function table for each function. Then, graph the function.

a

b

1. $y = x + 4$

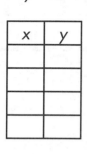

x	y

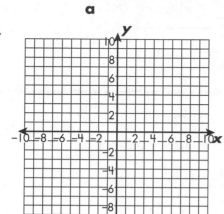

$y = 4x - 2$

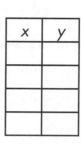

x	y

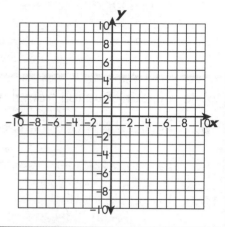

Graph the solution to each inequality.

2. $y < x + 2$

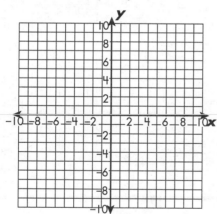

$y \geq 2x - 2$

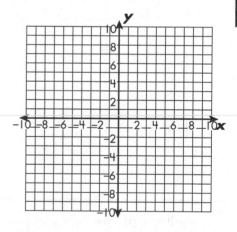

Answer each question.

3. What is the constant of proportionality in the table?

x	y
2	5
3	7.5
4	10

_____

4. If you know that the direct variation equation is $y = 4x$ and $y = 28$, what is x?

_____

5. Using the same equation, what is y if

$x = 6$? _____

Check What You Learned

Functions and Graphing

6. Evan biked 8 miles in 30 minutes. Express his rate of speed as a direct variation equation, using d for distance and t for time (in hours). _____

7. At that rate, how long would it take him to bike 24 miles? _____

Write a linear equation from the information given below.

8. The slope is 4 and the line passes through point $(-2, -6)$. _____

9. The line passes through points $(0, 4)$ and $(-2, 2)$. _____

10. The function table for the line is shown below.

x	y
-2	-7
-1	-6
0	-5
1	-4
2	-3
3	-2

11. The graph for the line is shown below.

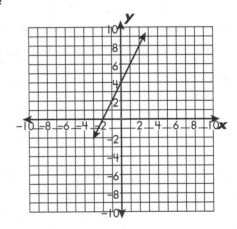

_____   _____

Use similar right triangles to prove that each line has a constant slope.

a

12.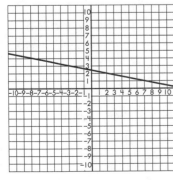

Triangle 1 Legs:

_____ & _____

Triangle 2 Legs:

_____ & _____

Proportionality Test:

b

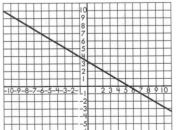

Triangle 1 Legs:

_____ & _____

Triangle 2 Legs:

_____ & _____

Proportionality Test:

Check What You Learned

Functions and Graphing

Decide if each table represents a function by stating *yes* or *no*.

a

13.

input	output
3	4, 2
4	−6
5	−7
−2	5

_____

b

input	output
−4	6
−3	2
1	0
7	6

_____

c

input	output
−3	4
−2	5
0	0
4	8

_____

Find the relationship for each function table and then complete the table.

a

14.

x	y
3	
4	40
9	
10	94

Function: _____

b

x	y
14	−3
63	
70	
77	6

Function: _____

Find the rate of change, or slope, for points on the function table and decide if it represents a *linear* or *nonlinear* relationship.

15.

x	y	Rate
0	14	
2	10	
3	8	
5	12	

Relationship: _____

x	y	Rate
−2	−17	
−1	−11	
0	−5	
1	1	

Relationship: _____

Compare the rate of change for the equation and table and decide which has a greater rate of change by writing *equation* or *table*.

16. $y = 6x - 2$ or

x	−3	2	6
y	5	−5	−13

_____

Check What You Know

Systems of Equations

Solve each system of equations.

	a	**b**

1.

$-4x - 15y = -17$

$-x + 5y = -13$

$x =$ _____, $y =$ _____

$-x - 7y = 14$

$-4x - 14y = 28$

$x =$ _____, $y =$ _____

2.

$y = -1\frac{1}{8} - \frac{7}{8}x$

$-4x + 9y = -22$

$x =$ _____, $y =$ _____

$y = \frac{1}{3}x + 2$

$5x + 4y = -30$

$x =$ _____, $y =$ _____

Use slope-intercept form to graph each system of equations and solve the system.

3. $y = 2x + 3$

$y = 3$

$x:$ _____,

$y:$ _____

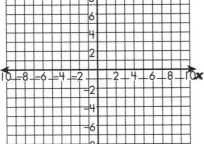

$y = \frac{1}{2}x + 4$

$y = x - 2$

$x:$ _____,

$y:$ _____

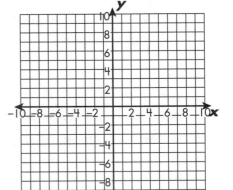

Set up a system of equations to solve the word problem.

4. At Billy's school, 80 students come to school by bicycle or by car. Together, the vehicles they arrive to school in have 270 wheels. How many of each are used? Use b to represent the number of bicycles and c to represent the number of cars.

Equation 1: _____

Equation 2: _____

$b =$ _____, $c =$ _____

Check What You Know

Systems of Equations

Solve each system of equations.

a	**b**	**c**
5. $y = \frac{5}{3}x - 1$	$6x + 4y = 6$	$y = \frac{1}{3}x - 4$
$y = -6$	$3x = -15$	$y = -\frac{7}{3}x + 4$
$x = $ _____, $y = $ _____	$x = $ _____, $y = $ _____	$x = $ _____, $y = $ _____

Graph the systems of equations.

6. $y = \frac{7}{4}x - 3$
   $y = 4$

7. $2x - y = 4$
   $x - y = 2$

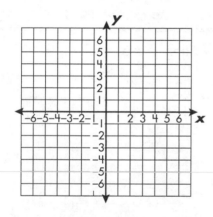

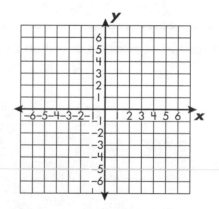

Use substitution or elimination to solve each system of equations.

a	**b**
8. $y = 3 - x$	$-4x + 9y = 9$
$y - 3x = 5$	$x = -6 + 3y$
$x = $ _____, $y = $ _____	$x = $ _____, $y = $ _____
9. $3g + f = 15$	$3b + 5t = 17$
$g + 2f = 10$	$2b + t = 9$
$g = $ _____, $f = $ _____	$b = $ _____, $t = $ _____

Lesson 9.1 Understanding Linear Equation Systems

A system of linear equations is a set of equations that have the same variables. Graphing the solutions of the equations results in a set of lines in the coordinate plane. If the lines intersect at a single point, that point represents the one ordered pair that satisfies the equation.

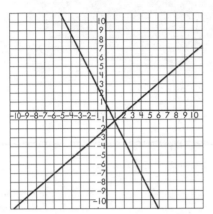

This represents a system because the lines intersect.

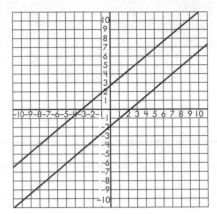

This is not a system because the lines do not intersect.

Tell if each graph represents a system of linear equations by writing *yes* or *no*.

a	b

1.

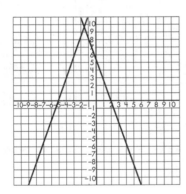

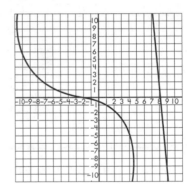

_____   _____

2.

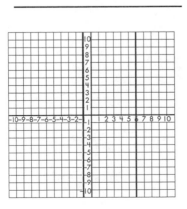

_____   _____

Lesson 9.2 Solving 2-Variable Linear Equation Systems

Systems of equations can be solved by using the method of substitution following the steps below.

$y = 7x + 10$
$y = 9x + 38$

$7x + 10 = 9x + 38$

$7x + 10 - 7x = 9x + 38 - 7x$

$10 = 2x + 38$

$10 - 38 = 2x + 38 - 38$

$-28 = 2x$

$-28 \div 2 = 2x \div 2$

$x = -14$

$y = 7(-14) + 10$

$y = -98 + 10$

$y = -88$

Step 1: Substitute one value of y so that there is only one variable in the new equation.

Step 2: Use the inverse operation and combine like terms with the x variable.

Step 3: Use the inverse operation to narrow the equation to 2 terms.

Step 4: Use the inverse operation to isolate the x variable.

Step 5: Find the value of the x variable.

Step 6: Substitute the value of the x variable in one of the equations.

Step 7: Solve to find the value of the y variable.

Use substitution to solve each equation system.

a

b

1.
$y = -\frac{4}{3}x + 6$

$y = 2$

$x = \underline{\hspace{1cm}}, y = \underline{\hspace{1cm}}$

$y = \frac{1}{2}x + 3$

$y = 5$

$x = \underline{\hspace{1cm}}, y = \underline{\hspace{1cm}}$

2.
$y = 4x + 5$

$y = -\frac{1}{3}x - 8$

$x = \underline{\hspace{1cm}}, y = \underline{\hspace{1cm}}$

$y = \frac{7}{2}x - 5$

$y = -5$

$x = \underline{\hspace{1cm}}, y = \underline{\hspace{1cm}}$

3.
$y = \frac{1}{3}x - 4$

$y = -\frac{7}{3}x + 4$

$x = \underline{\hspace{1cm}}, y = \underline{\hspace{1cm}}$

$y = -\frac{5}{2}x + 10$

$y = \frac{1}{2}x + 4$

$x = \underline{\hspace{1cm}}, y = \underline{\hspace{1cm}}$

Lesson 9.2 Solving 2-Variable Linear Equation Systems

Systems of equations can be solved by using the method of elimination following the steps below.

$$3x + 4y = 31$$
$$2x - y = 6$$

$$2x - y = 6$$
$$2x - y - 2x = 6 - 2x$$
$$-y = 6 - 2x$$
$$y = -6 + 2x$$
$$3x + 4(-6 + 2x) = 31$$
$$3x - 24 + 8x = 31$$
$$11x - 24 = 31$$
$$11x - 24 + 24 = 31 + 24$$
$$11x = 55$$
$$11x \div 11 = 55 \div 11$$
$$x = 5$$
$$y = -6 - 2(5)$$
$$y = -16$$

Step 1: Use inverse operations to isolate one variable on one side of the equation.

Step 2: Substitute the new equation in place of the appropriate variable so there is only one variable in the new equation.

Step 3: Use inverse operations and the distributive property to find a solution for the variable.

Step 4: Substitute the value of the variable in one of the equations and solve.

Use elimination to solve each system of equations.

	a	**b**

1.

$$-4x - 2y = -12$$
$$4x + 8y = -24$$
$$x = \_\_\_\_\_, y = \_\_\_\_\_$$

$$4x + 8y = 20$$
$$-4x + 2y = -30$$
$$x = \_\_\_\_\_, y = \_\_\_\_\_$$

2.

$$x - y = 11$$
$$2x + y = 19$$
$$x = \_\_\_\_\_, y = \_\_\_\_\_$$

$$-6x + 5y = 1$$
$$6x + 4y = -10$$
$$x = \_\_\_\_\_, y = \_\_\_\_\_$$

3.

$$-2x - 9y = -25$$
$$-4x - 9y = -23$$
$$x = \_\_\_\_\_, y = \_\_\_\_\_$$

$$8x + y = -16$$
$$-3x + y = -5$$
$$x = \_\_\_\_\_, y = \_\_\_\_\_$$

Lesson 9.3 Graphing Linear Equation Systems

Graphing both lines that make up an equation system can solve the system.

$$y = 3x + 2$$
$$y = 2x + 1$$

Step 1: Graph the first line in the system using slope intercept form as a guide.

Step 2: Graph the second line in the system using slope-intercept form as a guide.

Step 3: Find the point of intersection to solve the equation system.

$$(-1, -1)$$

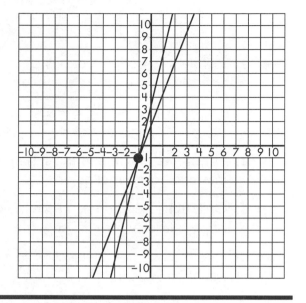

Use slope-intercept form to graph each system of equations and solve the system.

a   **b**

1. $y = -x + 4$

$y = 3x$

x: _____,

y: _____

$y = 2x + 4$

$y = 3x + 2$

x: _____,

y: _____

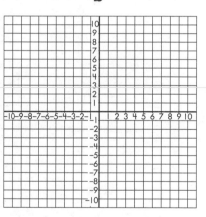

2. $y = -2x - 4$

$y = -4$

x: _____,

y: _____

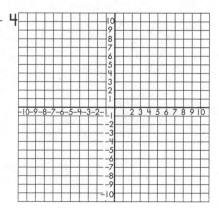

$y = 2x - 2$

$y = -x - 5$

x: _____,

y: _____

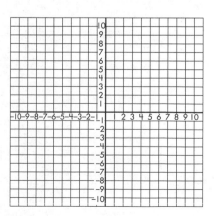

Lesson 9.3 Graphing Linear Equation Systems

In some cases, you must first isolate the y before you can solve the system.

$$2x - 4y = 10$$
$$x + y = 2$$

Step 1: Isolate y in both equations by using inverse operations to create slope-intercept form.

$$y = \frac{1}{2}x - 2\frac{1}{2}$$
$$y = -x + 2$$

Step 2: Graph the first line in the system using slope intercept form as a guide.

Step 3: Graph the second line in the system using slope-intercept form as a guide.

Step 4: Find the point of intersection to solve the equation system.

$$(3, -1)$$

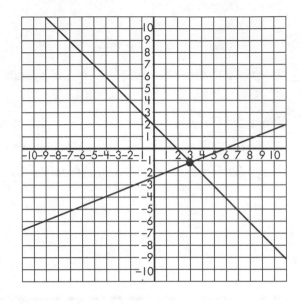

Use slope-intercept form to graph each system of equations and solve the system.

a   **b**

1. $x + y = 2$

$-9x + 4y = 8$

$x:$ _____,

$y:$ _____

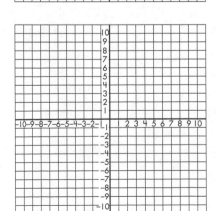

$5x + y = 9$

$10x - 7y = -18$

$x:$ _____,

$y:$ _____

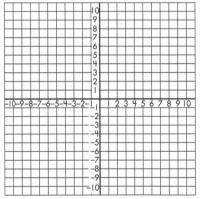

2. $2x - y = 0$

$x + y = -6$

$x:$ _____,

$y:$ _____

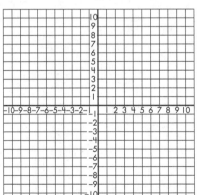

$x - 3y = 2$

$2x + 5y = 15$

$x:$ _____,

$y:$ _____

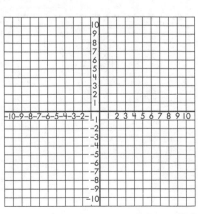

Lesson 9.4 Problem-Solving With Linear Equation Systems

Linear equation systems can be used to find solutions to word problems that have a constant relationship between two variables.

The admission fee at a fair is $2.00 for children and $5.00 for adults. On a certain day, 2,400 people enter the fair and $6,801 is collected. How many children and how many adults went to the fair that day? Use a to represent the number of adults and c to represent the number of children.

$$a + c = 2400$$
$$5a + 2c = 6801$$

$$a = 2400 - c$$
$$5(2400 - c) + 2c = 6801$$
$$12,000 - 5c + 2c = 6801$$
$$12,000 - 3c = 6801$$
$$12,000 - 3c - 12,000 = 6801 - 12,000$$
$$-3c \div (-3) = -5199 \div (-3)$$
$$c = 1,733$$
$$a + 1733 = 2400$$
$$a + 1733 - 1733 = 2400 - 1733$$
$$a = 667$$

667 adults and 1,733 children went to the fair that day.

Step 1: Use the word problem to set up the system of equations.

Step 2: Use the simplest equation to isolate one variable.

Step 3: Use substitution to replace one of variables.

Step 4: Use combination of like terms and inverse operations to isolate the variable in the equation.

Step 5: Find the value of one variable.

Step 6: Use the value of the first variable in the simplest equation to find the value of the second variable.

Set up a system of equations to solve each word problem.

1. At a convenience store, bottled water costs $1.10 and sodas cost $2.35. One day, the receipts for a total of 172 waters and sodas were $294.20. How many of each kind were sold? Use w to represent bottled water and s to represent soda.

Equation 1: _____

Equation 2: _____

$w =$ _____, $s =$ _____

2. Your teacher is giving you a test worth 100 points that contains 40 questions. There are 2-point questions and 4-point questions on the test. How many of each type of question are on the test? Use t to represent 2-point questions and f to represent 4-point questions.

Equation 1: _____

Equation 2: _____

$t =$ _____, $f =$ _____

NAME _____

 Check What You Learned

Systems of Equations

Solve each system of equations.

a

b

1.

$$-4x - 2y = 14$$

$$-10x + 7y = -25$$

x = _____, y = _____

$$y = \frac{3}{2}x - 2$$

$$y = x + 2$$

x = _____, y = _____

2.

$$5x + 4y = -14$$

$$y = 1 - \frac{1}{2}x$$

x = _____, y = _____

$$-20y - 7x = -14$$

$$10y - 2x = -4$$

x = _____, y = _____

Use slope-intercept form to graph each system of equations and solve the system.

3. $-2x + 5y = 15$

$y = -x - 4$

x: _____,

y: _____

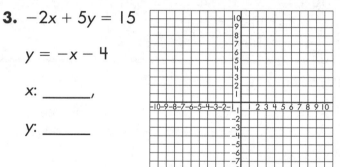

$-x + 5y = 40$

$8x + 4y = -12$

x: _____,

y: _____

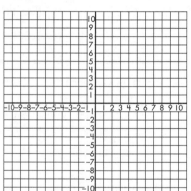

Set up a system of equations to solve the word problem.

4. Kim scored 33 points at her basketball game with a combination of 2-point shots and 3-point shots. If she made a total of 15 baskets, how many of each kind of shot did Kim make? Use *t* to represent 2-point shots and *x* to represent 3-point shots.

Equation 1: _____

Equation 2: _____   t = _____, x = _____

Spectrum Algebra
Grades 6–8
102

Check What You Learned
Chapter 9

Check What You Learned

Systems of Equations

Set up a system of equations to solve each word problem.

5. Last Saturday 2,200 people attended an event at Fairway Gardens. The admission fee was $1.50 for children and $4.00 for adults. If the total amount of money collected at the event was $5,050, how many children and how many adults attended the event? Use c to represent the number of children and a to represent the number of adults.

Equation 1: _____   Equation 2: _____

$c =$ _____, $a =$ _____

Use substitution or elimination to solve each system of equations.

	a	**b**	**c**
6.	$y = -\frac{1}{2}x + 18$	$y = x - 11$	$-8x + 2y = -48$
	$y = -x + 20$	$4x + \frac{4}{5}y = 68$	$6x - 2y = 28$
	$x =$ ____, $y =$ ____	$x =$ ____, $y =$ ____	$x =$ ____, $y =$ ____

Use slope-intercept form to graph each system of equations and solve the system.

a

7. $y = -2x - 3$

$y = 2x$

$x:$ _____,

$y:$ _____

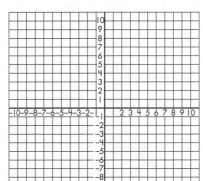

b

$y = \frac{3}{4}x - 3$

$y = -\frac{1}{2}x + 2$

$x:$ _____,

$y:$ _____

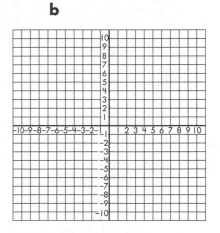

Final Test Chapters 1–9

Create expressions equivalent to the ones below.

1. $2(9x + 3^2)$ _____

2. $5^3(2 + 4c)$ _____

3. $\frac{x + x}{3}$ _____

Solve each problem. Write each answer in simplest form.

4. Katie has $16\frac{3}{4}$ hours to finish 3 school projects. How much time may she spend on each project, if she plans to spend the same amount of time on each?

   Katie will spend _____ hours on each project.

5. Martha spent $2.90 on $3\frac{1}{2}$ pounds of bananas. How much did she spend on each pound of bananas?

   She spent _____ on each pound.

Solve each problem.

6. Alicia had $22 to spend on pencils. If each pencil costs $1.50, how many pencils can she buy? Let p represent the cost of each pencil.

   Equation or Inequality: _____

   Alicia can buy _____ pencils.

7. The sum of three consecutive numbers is 51. What is the smallest of these numbers? Let n represent the smallest number of the set.

   Equation or Inequality: _____

   The smallest of these numbers is _____.

8. On Tuesday, Shanice bought 5 new pens. On Wednesday, half of all the pens that she had were accidentally thrown away. On Thursday, there were only 16 left. How many did she have on Monday? Let p represent the number of pens she had on Monday.

   Equation or inequality: _____

   Shanice had _____ pens on Monday.

Final Test Chapters 1–9

Solve the following equations. Write each answer in simplest form.

	a	**b**	**c**
9.	$-2.4n = 13.2$ _____	$\frac{p}{8} = 6$ _____	$18 = 2k - 4$ _____

Solve each equation. Write *null* or *all*, if appropriate.

	a	**b**
10.	$\frac{4w}{2} = w + 2$ _____	$6.4c - 8 = c + 13.6$ _____
11.	$3(6 + 2n) = 5(n + 7)$ _____	$24m + 4 = 4(1 + 6m)$ _____
12.	$2(p - 4) = 25 - p$ _____	$3(5 + 3y) = 9y - 11$ _____

Write an equation or inequality for each problem. Use n as the variable. Then, solve the equation or inequality.

13. Kiara bought 3 T-shirts. Each cost $15. She also paid a tax of 5% of the cost. How much did she spend in total?

Equation _____   Kiara spent a total of $_____.

14. Raul set aside $320 for workout classes at a gym. The membership costs $250. He must pay $5 for each class he attends. How many classes can he attend without going over his budget?

Inequality _____   Solution: _____

Write a linear equation for the information given below.

15. The slope is 8 and the line passes through point $(4, -2)$. _____

16. The line passes through points $(-4, 6)$ and $(4, 14)$. _____

Rewrite each expression using a base and an exponent.

17. $3^5 \times 3^{-4} =$ _____ $8^{-6} \div 8^{-3} =$ _____

18. $2^6 \div 2^8 =$ _____ $4^2 \times 4^4 =$ _____

Final Test Chapters 1–9

Complete the function table for each function. Then, graph the function.

a   **b**

19. $y = \frac{x}{2} + 1$ $y = 2x - 4$

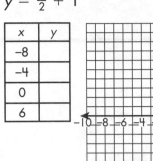

x	y
−8	
−4	
0	
6	

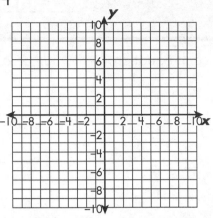

x	y
−2	
0	
3	
5	

---

20. Maia walked 5.25 miles in 1.5 hours. Express her rate of speed as a direct variation equation. Use *d* for distance and *t* for time. _____

Create a scatterplot from the data below.

21. (0, 45), (1, 50), (2, 60), (3, 75), (4, 95)

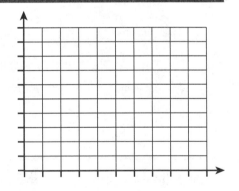

---

22. What are the coordinates of the preimage?

A (_____), B (_____), C (_____)

23. What are the coordinates of the image?

A′ (_____), B′ (_____), C′ (_____)

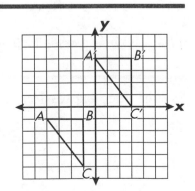

Final Test Chapters 1–9

Solve this problem.

24. Jon has a photograph that measures 4 inches wide by 6 inches long. He asked a photo shop to reproduce the photo 25% larger. What will the new dimensions be?

New width: _____ in.   New length: _____ in.

Use substitution or elimination to solve each system of equations.

	a			**b**	

25. $y = \frac{2}{3}x - 5$ $x =$ _____, $x + y = -3$ $x =$ _____,

 $y = -x + 10$ $y =$ _____ $x - y = 1$ $y =$ _____

26. $3x - y = 0$ $x =$ _____, $-6x + 6y = 6$ $x =$ _____,

 $\frac{1}{4}x + \frac{3}{4}y = \frac{5}{2}$ $y =$ _____ $-6x + 3y = -12$ $y =$ _____

Set up a system of equations to solve each word problem.

27. Jonathan has saved 57 coins in his bank. The coins are a mixture of quarters and dimes. He has saved $12.00 so far. How many quarters and how many dimes are in Jonathan's bank? Use q to represent the number of quarters and d to represent the number of dimes.

Equation 1: _____   Equation 2: _____

$q =$ _____, $d =$ _____

Use similar right triangles to prove that each line has a constant slope.

28.

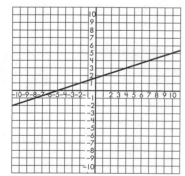

Triangle 1 Legs:

_____ & _____

Triangle 2 Legs:

_____ & _____

Proportionality Test:

 ___ = ___

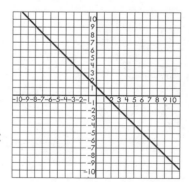

Triangle 1 Legs:

_____ & _____

Triangle 2 Legs:

_____ & _____

Proportionality Test:

___ = ___

Algebra Reference Chart

Number Properties	
Commutative Properties of Addition and Multiplication	$a + b = b + a$ $a \times b = b \times a$
Associative Properties of Addition and Multiplication	$(a + b) + c = a + (b + c)$ $(a \times b) \times c = a \times (b \times c)$
Identity Properties of Addition and Multiplication	$a + 0 = a$ $a \times 1 = a$
Properties of Zero	$a \times 0 = 0 \qquad 0 \div a = 0$
Distributive Property	$a \times (b + c) = (a \times b) + (a \times c)$

Formulas	
Perimeter of a rectangle	$P = 2l + 2w$
Area of a rectangle	$A = lw$
Perimeter of a square	$P = 4s$
Perimeter of a triangle	$P = a + b + c$
Area of a triangle	$A = \frac{1}{2} bh$
Area of a circle	$A = \pi r^2$
Circumference of a circle	$C = 2\pi r \ (\pi = 3.14)$

Pythagorean Theorem

$$a^2 + b^2 = c^2$$

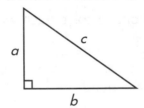

Triangles

equilateral   isosceles   scalene

right angle   obtuse angle   acute angle

 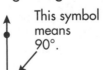 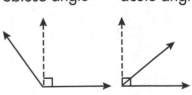

This symbol means 90°.

Table of Squares and Square Roots

Except in the case of perfect squares, square roots shown on the chart are not exact.

Table of Squares and Square Roots

n	n^2	$\sqrt{n}$	n	n^2	$\sqrt{n}$
1	1	1	51	2,601	7.14
2	4	1.41	52	2,704	7.21
3	9	1.73	53	2,809	7.28
4	16	2	54	2,916	7.35
5	25	2.24	55	3,025	7.42
6	36	2.45	56	3,136	7.48
7	49	2.65	57	3,249	7.55
8	64	2.83	58	3,364	7.62
9	81	3	59	3,481	7.68
10	100	3.16	60	3,600	7.75
11	121	3.32	61	3,721	7.81
12	144	3.46	62	3,844	7.87
13	169	3.61	63	3,969	7.94
14	196	3.74	64	4,096	8
15	225	3.87	65	4,225	8.06
16	256	4	66	4,356	8.12
17	289	4.12	67	4,489	8.19
18	324	4.24	68	4,624	8.25
19	361	4.36	69	4,761	8.31
20	400	4.47	70	4,900	8.37
21	441	4.58	71	5,041	8.43
22	484	4.69	72	5,184	8.49
23	529	4.80	73	5,329	8.54
24	576	4.90	74	5,476	8.60
25	625	5	75	5,625	8.66
26	676	5.10	76	5,776	8.72
27	729	5.20	77	5,929	8.77
28	784	5.29	78	6,084	8.83
29	841	5.39	79	6,241	8.89
30	900	5.48	80	6,400	8.94
31	961	5.57	81	6,561	9
32	1,024	5.66	82	6,724	9.06
33	1,089	5.74	83	6,889	9.11
34	1,156	5.83	84	7,056	9.17
35	1,225	5.92	85	7,225	9.22
36	1,296	6	86	7,396	9.27
37	1,369	6.08	87	7,569	9.33
38	1,444	6.16	88	7,744	9.38
39	1,521	6.24	89	7,921	9.43
40	1,600	6.32	90	8,100	9.49
41	1,681	6.40	91	8,281	9.54
42	1,764	6.48	92	8,464	9.59
43	1,849	6.56	93	8,649	9.64
44	1,936	6.63	94	8,836	9.70
45	2,025	6.71	95	9,025	9.75
46	2,116	6.78	96	9,216	9.80
47	2,209	6.86	97	9,409	9.85
48	2,304	6.93	98	9,604	9.90
49	2,401	7	99	9,801	9.95
50	2,500	7.07	100	10,000	10

Scoring Record for Posttests, Mid-Test, and Final Test

Chapter Posttest	Your Score	Performance			
		Excellent	Very Good	Fair	Needs Improvement
1	____ of 43	39–43	35–38	31–34	30 or fewer
2	____ of 43	39–43	35–38	31–34	30 or fewer
3	____ of 43	39–43	35–38	31–34	30 or fewer
4	____ of 39	36–39	32–35	28–31	27 or fewer
5	____ of 27	25–27	22–24	20–21	19 or fewer
6	____ of 16	15–16	13–14	11–12	10 or fewer
7	____ of 34	31–34	28–30	24–27	23 or fewer
8	____ of 23	22–23	19–21	17–18	16 or fewer
9	____ of 13	12–13	10–11	9	8 or fewer
Mid-Test	____ of 83	75–83	67–74	58–66	57 or fewer
Final Test	____ of 39	36–39	32–35	28–31	27 or fewer

Record your test score in the Your Score column. See where your score falls in the Performance columns. Your score is based on the total number of required responses. If your score is fair or needs improvement, review the chapter material.

Algebra Answers

Chapter 1

Check What You Know, page 1

	a	b
1.	$x - 3$	$n \div 7$
2.	10×9	$a + 5$
3.	$3 \times n = 12$	$n - 5 = 7$
4.	$n + 2 < 10$	$18 \div n = 6$
5.	seven increased by n	Three times n, plus two, is twenty-nine.

6. $4 \times (8 - 3)$
7. $4 + (5 \times 3)$
8. $16 - (4 \times 2)$
9. $(25 \div 5) + 3$
10. $(6 \times 2) - 1$

11.	$8 + 9$	$(5 \times 3) \times 4$
12.	91	0

Check What You Know, page 2

	a	b
13.	49	13
14.	43	35
15.	A	

	a	b	c
16.	8	2	2
17.	16	1	25
18.	$1\frac{1}{2}$	36	3
19.	100	5	9

20. $3s = 48$; $16; $16, $32
21. the number of men; $23 - n = 5$ or $n + 5 = 23$; 18; 18

Lesson 1.1, page 3

	a	b
1.	$x + 2$	$11 - 4$
2.	9×8	$10 + r$
3.	$b \div 5$	3×7
4.	$s - 1$	$12 + 6$

5. two more than d, or two added to d, or d increased by two, or a number increased by two
6. three times n, or three ns, or the product of three and n, or the product of three and a number

Lesson 1.2, page 4

	a	b
1.	$3; x$	$4; y$
2.	$1; z$	$5; n$
3.	$n + 5$	$11 \times n$

4. $n \times 3 > 27$
5. $10 \div n = 2$
6. x divided by three is twelve, or a number divided by three is twelve.
7. Seven times n, plus three, is less than thirty-one; or seven times a number, plus three, is less than thirty-one.

Lesson 1.3, page 5

1.	identity	property of zero
2.	associative	identity
3.	commutative	property of zero
4.	y	$(6 \times 7) \times 8$
5.	$4 + 5$	0
6.	$(7 + b) + 9$	3×10

Lesson 1.4, page 6

1. Perform the operation inside parentheses first, $2[5 + 6 \div 2 - (7)]$. Then, perform division, $2[5 + 3 - 7]$. Then, perform addition and subtraction from left to right, $2[8 - 7]$. Finally, multiply the difference by the factor of 2, $2[1] = 2$.

	a	b
2.	10	2
3.	3	7
4.	45	19
5.	45	54
6.	11	36
7.	15	3

Lesson 1.5, page 7

1. $A\,(2, 2)$; $B\,(-2, -5)$
2. $C\,(-6, 4)$; $D\,(3, -6)$
3. $G\,(-4, -3)$; $H\,(4, -4)$
4. $I\,(-6, 5)$; $J\,(5, -8)$
5. **Grid 1**

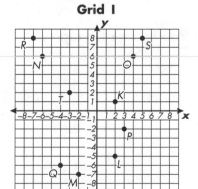

Lesson 1.5, page 8

1.

Tubs (x values)	Dollars (y values)
100	500
200	1,000
300	1,500
400	2,000

Algebra Answers

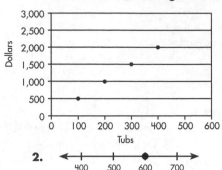

Profit from Cookie Dough Sales

2. ◄──┼────┼───◆───┼──►
        400   500   600   700

Check What You Learned, page 9

	a	b
1.	$b \div 3$	$7 \times n$
2.	$42 - 10$	$7 - n$
3.	$7 - 3 = 4$	$12 \div n = 3$
4.	$x - 6 > 10$	$5 \times b = 20$
5.	b increased by twenty-two;	Two times b, plus seven, is fifteen.
6.	$3 + b$	$8 \times (f + 7)$
7.	$8 \times d$	$p + 4 = 9$
8.	0	88
9.	$(2 + 4) + 5$	8×6
10.	$11 - n = 7$	
11.	$8n + 4 = 84$	
12.	$n \div 5 = 6$	

Check What You Learned, page 10

	a	b
13.	14	8
14.	11	3
15.	18	15
16.	$A\,(6, 4)$	$B\,(-3, 1)$
17.	$C\,(-6, -6)$	$D\,(3, -5)$
18.		

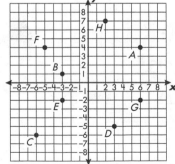

19. $(3, 1)$
20. 6 units

	a	b
21.	$(3 \times d) - 8$	$x - 3$
22.	$g - 2 = 14$	$z + 8$

23. 9 divided by x
24. the product of 3 and g is 27

Chapter 2

Check What You Know, page 11

	a	b	c	d
1.	8	-8	2	-2
2.	2	-8	8	-2
3.	-6	0	0	6
4.	0	-16	16	0
5.	3	-3	-3	3
6.	-5	5	-1	1

	a	b
7.	$(4 \times 6) + (4 \times 7)$	$2 \times (3 + 5)$
8.	$(6 \times 4) - (6 \times 3)$	$4 \times (8 - 9)$

Check What You Know, page 12

	a	b	c
9.	7	12	4
10.	23	55	46
11.	19	5	11
12.	9	9	7
13.	20	4	51
14.	5	27	0
15.	2	3	40

16. $21 = 9 + x$; 12
17. $160 = 8x$; 20
18. -3.5

Lesson 2.1, page 13

	a	b	c
1.	6	-6	-2
2.	2	-6	6

3. ◄──┼──┼──┼──► ◄──┼──┼──┼──►
      -6 0 6 -2 0 2

4. ◄──┼──┼──┼──┼──┼──◆──┼──►
     -3 -2 -1 0   1   2   3

5. ◄──┼──◆──┼──┼──┼──┼──┼──►
     -3 -2 -1 0   1   2   3

Lesson 2.2, page 14

	a	b	c
1.	12	-35	-36
2.	3	-4	-5
3.	-72	-42	36
4.	-8	-4	-5
5.	-51	7	-108
6.	-18	-7	11
7.	20	-50	72
8.	-3	4	2
9.	88		
10.	$-\$10$		

Algebra Answers

Lesson 2.3, page 15

	a	b
1.	$(5 \times 3) + (5 \times 4)$	$3 \times (4 + 6)$
2.	$(15 \times 7) - (15 \times 4)$	$5 \times (6 - 7)$
3.	$3 \times (5 + 3)$	$5 \times (2x + 3)$
4.	$9a + 32$	
5.	$b + 12$	

Lesson 2.4, page 16

	a	b	c
1.	5	8	11
2.	19	31	10
3.	34	101	13
4.	12	18	6

5. $6 = 2 + 1 + x$; 3; Yes, 3 batches is reasonable because a total of 6 were made.
6. $15 = x - 3$; 18; Yes, 18 CDs is reasonable because it is close to Austin's number of CDs, 15.

Lesson 2.5, page 17

	a	b	c
1.	3	3	5
2.	22	7	26
3.	20	0	7
4.	12	9	30

5. $6.25 = 1.25x$; 5
6. $12 = 3x$; 4; Yes, 4 comic books is reasonable because it is the number of Luis's comic books divided by 3.

Lesson 2.6, page 18

	a	b	c
1.	3	16	3
2.	12	9	4
3.	5	5	11

4. $9 = \frac{x}{2} + 4$; $10
5. $9 = 2x + x + 3$; 2

Check What You Learned, page 19

	a	b	c	d
1.	24	−24	2	−2
2.				

```
<----+--+--+--+--+--●--+--+--+--+---->
     0  1  2  3  4  5  6  7  8  9  10
```

3.	65 °F			
4.	3	−3	−3	3
5.	−6	6	−1	1

6. $3x \times (9 + 8)$
7. $0.5(n + 5)$
8. $23a + 18$
9. $-21b + 84$
10. $17c + 2$

Check What You Learned, page 20

	a	b	c
11.	8	18	4
12.	13	31	59
13.	11	−7	11
14.	8	6	12
15.	30	9	52
16.	5	28	0
17.	5	4	12

18. $-9x = -54$ or $9x - 54 = 0$; 6
19. $33 = 3x$; $11;
    $3 \times 11 = 33$, so the answer is reasonable.
20. $5x = 20 - 7.50$; $2.50;
    $2.5 \times 5 = 12.5$, and $12.5 + 7.5 = 20$, so the answer is reasonable.

Chapter 3

Check What You Know, page 21

	a	b	c
1.	3	9	14
2.	5	12	12
3.	13	19	16
4.	2, 2, 13	2, 7, 7	2, 2, 3, 3, 3
5.	4.2×10^{-3}	4.2×10^2	4.2×10^4
6.	6×10^5	7×10^2	9×10^1

Check What You Know, page 22

	a	b
8.	$\frac{b}{a}$	$\frac{1}{2x}$
9.	OK	$10c$

10. $1,000 \times 1.02^{10}$; $1218.99
11. 3^5; 5^9
12. $\frac{1}{6^5}$; $\frac{1}{4^2}$
13. $225
14. $\frac{1}{8}$

Lesson 3.1, page 23

1. $9 = 1, 3, 9$;
   $15 = 1, 3, 5, 15$;
   Common = 1, 3; GCF = 3
2. $30 = 1, 2, 3, 5, 6, 10, 15, 30$;
   $48 = 1, 2, 3, 4, 6, 8, 12, 16, 24, 48$;
   Common = 1, 2, 3, 6; GCF = 6
3. $8 = 1, 2, 4, 8$
   $12 = 1, 2, 3, 4, 6, 12$
   Common = 1, 2, 4; GCF = 4
4. $6 = 1, 2, 3, 6$
   $18 = 1, 2, 3, 6, 9, 18$
   Common = 1, 2, 3, 6; GCF = 6

Algebra Answers

Lesson 3.2, page 24

	a	b
1.	17	36
2.	87	64
3.	810	1,296
4.	48	3,150
5.	1,584	64
6.	2,744	2
7.	9	22
8.	33,280	1

Lesson 3.3, page 25

	a	b
1.	x^2	OK
2.	$\frac{7}{5x}$	n^2
3.	$\frac{9t^3}{s}$	$\frac{8f^3}{g}$
4.	OK	1
5.	$\frac{t^4}{6}$	$\frac{b^2}{3}$
6.	$\frac{1}{2x}$	$\frac{2}{3y}$
7.	$\frac{1}{c}$	$\frac{4}{5ab}$
8.	$\frac{5n}{11}$	$\frac{7c}{13ab}$
9.	OK	$\frac{2r}{5}$
10.	$\frac{b}{10}$	$\frac{2pq}{9}$

Lesson 3.4, page 26

	a	b
1.	4^5	7^5
2.	8^2	4^4
3.	3^8	6^4
4.	9^3	8^6
5.	5^2	12^4
6.	5^4	10^7
7.	2^8	3^5
8.	11^3	2^2
9.	3000×1.02^{10}; 3,657	
10.	1.02^5	

Lesson 3.5, page 27

	a	b
1.	10^{-16}	9^8
2.	2^{-1}	6^{-9}
3.	3^{-5}	2^{-8}
4.	5^{-9}	7^1
5.	12^{-6}	8^9
6.	6^{-2}	11^{-7}
7.	2^{-1}	7^5
8.	4^2	12^{-10}
9.	2.5×10^{-1}	10. 10

Lesson 3.6, page 28

	a	b	c
1.	3.84×10	6.21×10^3	3.1×10^{-2}
2.	4.7165×10^4	7.6×10^{-4}	3.6732×10^2
3.	7.95×10^{-1}	9.215×10^2	6.1321×10^4
4.	0.0000417	2,070	0.000936
5.	955	0.0626	81,300
6.	0.576	757,000	0.0037
7.	3.844×10^5		
8.	1.5×10^8		

Check What You Learned, page 29

	a	b	c
1.	15^2	5^6	9^4
2.	17^1	s^3	q^5
3.	64	169	23
4.	64	1	10,000
5.	2.7×10^{-3}	2.7×10	2.7×10^3
6.	3×10	4×10^{-3}	5×10^4
7.	5×10^5	9×10^2	2.56×10^{-2}
8.	3.7×10^{-3}	1×10^5	4×10^2
9.	61,400	0.0614	0.000614

Check What You Learned, page 30

	a	b	c
10.	141	144	22
11.	32	990	6

	a	b
12.	OK	$\frac{2}{3n}$
13.	$\frac{1}{12b}$	$\frac{abc}{3}$
14.	8^{15}	3^2
15.	3^{-2}	11^{12}
16.	$1,500 \times 1.03^5$; $1,738.91	
17.	10^3 dm or 1,000 dm	

Chapter 4

Check What You Know, page 31

	a	b	c
1.	7	6	15
2.	14	2	22
3.	33	13	0
4.	−13	0	15
5.	4.5	15.3	$\frac{1}{14}$
6.	$\frac{1}{72}$	$-26\frac{2}{3}$	3
7.	$7\frac{7}{12}$		
8.	$2,599.50		

Algebra Answers

Check What You Know, page 32

	a	b	c
1.	5	3	10
2.	$\frac{2}{4}$	9	$\frac{3}{5}$
3.	3; 4		
4.	4; 5		
5.	8	81	7
6.	=	<	<

7.

Lesson 4.1, page 33

1. $\frac{3}{4}$; 0.75
2. $1\frac{1}{4}$; 1.25
3. $\frac{5}{18}$; $0.2\overline{7}$
4. $3\frac{3}{4}$; 3.75
5. $8\frac{1}{3}$; $8.\overline{3}$

Lesson 4.2, page 34

	a	b	c	d
1.	$11\frac{1}{2}$	$1\frac{8}{9}$	$5\frac{4}{5}$	$23\frac{2}{3}$
2.	$11\frac{1}{4}$	$9\frac{7}{15}$	$3\frac{1}{33}$	$7\frac{6}{7}$
3.	$\frac{13}{3}$	$\frac{49}{9}$	$\frac{14}{5}$	$\frac{23}{7}$
4.	$\frac{29}{4}$	$\frac{59}{6}$	$\frac{56}{9}$	$\frac{67}{8}$

Lesson 4.3, page 35

	a	b	c
1.	rational	irrational	rational
2.	rational	rational	rational
3.	rational	rational	rational
4.	irrational	rational	rational
5.	irrational	irrational	rational

Lesson 4.4, page 36

	a	b	c
1.	3	9	6
2.	5	2	8
3.	8; 9; 9		
4.	5; 6; 5		
5.	20	5	7
6.	2	4	10

Lesson 4.5, page 37

	a	b	c
1.	<	<	>
2.	>	=	<
3.	2.6; 2.7		
4.	3.1; 3.2		

5.

Lesson 4.6, page 38

	a	b	c
1.	2.4	19.8	15.6
2.	$\frac{1}{2}$	6	$\frac{1}{6}$
3.	-2	-0.95	3
4.	$\frac{1}{45}$	$-11\frac{3}{7}$	2
5.	$1\frac{1}{8}$ ft.		
6.	6.5 hours		

Check What You Learned, page 39

	a	b	c
1.	rational	irrational	irrational
2.	rational	irrational	irrational
3.	rational	rational	rational
4.	<	<	<
5.	>	<	<
6.	>	<	<
7.	2.23; 2.24		
8.	3.60; 3.61		

9.

Check What You Learned, page 40

	a	b	c
10.	0.4	0.52	0.172
11.	6.36	5.98	3.125

	a	b	c	d
12.	$12\frac{1}{2}$	$1\frac{4}{9}$	$10\frac{1}{5}$	$7\frac{1}{3}$
13.	$5\frac{5}{11}$	$4\frac{7}{10}$	$\frac{28}{3}$	$\frac{17}{2}$
14.	$\frac{37}{5}$	$\frac{47}{7}$	$\frac{45}{8}$	$\frac{41}{9}$

Chapter 5

Check What You Know, page 41

	a	b	c
1.	True		True
2.		True	
3.	5	24	5
4.	33	15	4
5.	20	14	8
6.	7	12	39
7.	30	48	3
8.	15	25	6
9.	12%	1%	40%
10.	406%	12.5%	60%

Algebra Answers

Check What You Know, page 42

11. 12
12. 11.98
13. $48.65
14. $194.60
15. 4%
16. 3 years
17. $168; $768
18. $3,500; $3,937.50
19. $265.99; $2,265.99
20. $32.48; $832.48

Lesson 5.1, page 43

	a	b	c
1.	True		True
2.		True	
3.	$\frac{3}{2}$		
4.			

Ice Cream	180	360	540	720	900	1,080
Hours	2	4	6	8	10	12

Lesson 5.2, page 44

1. 5
2. 100
3. $\frac{1}{2}$ hour

	a	b	c
4.	yes	yes	no
5.	no	yes	no

Lesson 5.3, page 45

	a	b	c
1.	$\frac{1}{5}$	37.5	$1\frac{1}{5}$
2.	262.5	$\frac{41}{50}$	$\frac{57}{400}$
3.	$1\frac{16}{25}$	35	16
4.	95	$2\frac{12}{25}$	330
5.	0.0575	12.5	0.58
6.	115	0.09	3.5
7.	2.25	0.5	0.99
8.	80	382	0.5225

Lesson 5.4, page 46

1. 22.50
2. 20
3. $59.50
4. $125
5. 480

Lesson 5.5, page 47

1. 5%
2. $1\frac{1}{2}$ years
3. $176
4. $6,500
5. 675
6. 4,000

Lesson 5.6, page 48

1. $3,401.22
2. $3,522.72
3. $1,607.79
4. $735.66
5. $541.21; $550

Check What You Learned, page 49

	a	b	c
1.	True	True	
2.	True		True
3.	no	yes	no
4.	yes	no	no
5.	160		
6.	105		
7.	35		

Check What You Learned, page 50

8. 8 miles
9. 5.85
10. $45
11.

Distance	650	1300	1950
Hours	3	6	9

12. $112.50; $862.50
13. $3000; $3090
14. $434.87; $4434.87
15. $84.93; $584.93

Mid-Test, page 51

	a	b	c
1.	p	$9 + (k + 3)$	
2.	$7n \times z$	$6(w + x)$	
3.	$8 \div -4$; 7	$(-6 + 3)$; -8	
4.	$15 \div 3$; 16	$(8 - 3)$; 1.25	
5.	$(2 + 6)$; -96	$(6 - 3)$; 132	
6.	72	91	9
7.	4	39	11
8.	0	90	7
9.	$6n = \$54$; $9.00		
10.	$(2n - 3) + n = 33$; Jack: 12; Dion: 21		

Algebra Answers

Mid-Test, page 52

	a	b	c
11.	(4, 8)	(−3, −8)	(−6, 6)

11–13.

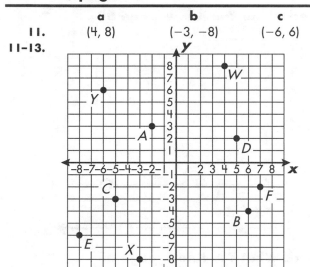

	a	b	c
14.	28	272	81
15.	100	8	39
16.	7^{-3}	4^{-8}	6^{12}
17.	7.564×10^3	8.97×10^{-2}	3.2857×10^4
18.	3×10	4×10^3	5×10^4
19.	6×10^5	7×10^2	9×10
20.	4×10^4	1×10^5	4×10^2

Mid-Test, page 53

	a	b	c
21.	−1.7	$\frac{1}{8}$	3.875
22.	$-5\frac{1}{3}$	$\frac{1}{6}$	$-\frac{1}{6}$
23.	$2\frac{1}{3} + \frac{3}{4} + 1\frac{1}{6} = n; 4\frac{1}{4}$		
24.	$6\frac{1}{4} \div 1\frac{1}{4} = n; 5$		
25.	14	6	32
26.	4	72	52
27.	13	12	−1
28.	15	14	55

Mid-Test, page 54

29.	17%
30.	$35.75
31.	15%
32.	$45
33.	6
34.	864
35.	12.5%
36.	8
37.	$749.18; $6749.18
38.	$31.14; $331.14

Chapter 6

Check What You Know, page 55

1.	$4a + 4b$
2.	$27a + 24b$
3.	$9x + 18y$
4.	$3\frac{1}{3}$
5.	$14\frac{5}{8}$
6.	$\frac{1}{10}$
7.	$8(4a + 7b)$
8.	$3(5y + 6x)$

Lesson 6.1, page 56

1.	$28z + 56b$
2.	$16x + 72$
3.	$4 \times 4r$
4.	$27 + 72x$
5.	$48 + 96t$
6.	$\frac{3t}{1}$
7.	$8s^3 + 4$
8.	$90x + 120$
9.	$30a + 54b$
10.	$27x + 486$
11.	$7(3c)$
12.	$18 + 63f$

Lesson 6.2, page 57

	a	b
1.	$4(m + 3)$	$2(x + 4y)$
2.	$9(t + 2)$	$5(2v - 3w)$
3.	$6(b - 3a)$	$14(3 + 5)$
4.	$7(2y + 5x)$	OK
5.	$13(3 + 7)$	$2(f + 24)$
6.	$x(1 - 51)$	$4(-s + 14)$
7.	$7(y + 8z)$	$5(p + 6q)$

Lesson 6.3, page 58

1.	$\frac{2}{3}$
2.	$14\frac{7}{12}$

3.	$a \div 5 = 9$	$k + \frac{1}{5}$
	$9 \times 5 = a$	$k + 0.2$

Algebra Answers

Lesson 6.4, page 59

1. $d = (4 \times 40) - (4 \times 32)$
   $d = 4 \times (40 - 32)$
   32
2. $s = 15 + 17 + 12$
   $s = 12 + 15 + 17$
   44
3. $m = 3 \times (\$1.25 + \$2.00)$
   $m = (3 \times \$1.25) + (3 \times \$2.00)$
   $9.75

Lesson 6.5, page 60

1. $1.5 \times n = 90$; 60; 30
2. $(2 \times n) - \frac{3}{4} = 5\frac{1}{4}$; 3 miles; $2\frac{1}{4}$ miles
3. $(2 \times n) + \$12 = \$98$; $43; $55

Lesson 6.6, page 61

1. total cost $= \$1.25 \times$ weight

Dependent Variable	Cost (Dollars)	$1.25	$2.50	$3.75
Independent Variable	Weight (Pounds)	1	2	3

2. height $= 6 + (2 \times$ time$)$

Dependent Variable	Height (Feet)	12	18	24
Independent Variable	Time (Years)	3	6	9

3. $y = \frac{1}{2}x$; 80 minutes

Check What You Learned, page 62

1. $4a + 4b$
2. $27a + 24b$
3. $9x + 18y$
4. $18x + 18$
5. $250 + 500c$
6. $\frac{2x}{3}$
7. $192 + 80c$
8. $238r + 459 - 7r$ or $231r + 459$
9. $6(n + 12)$
10. $3(t + 7s)$
11. $7(b - 6a)$
12. time $= 150 \div$ reading speed

Dependent Variable	Time	10	7.5	5
Independent Variable	Speed (pgs./day)	15	20	30

Check What You Learned, page 63

13. $11.99
14. $d = (5 \times 2.5) - (4 \times 2.5)$
    $d = 2.5 (5 - 4)$
    2.5
15. $r = 792 - 5[(15 \times 5) + (25 \times 2)]$; 167
16. $y = 3x$; 8 hours

Chapter 7

Check What You Know, page 64

	a	b
1.	15	$\frac{1}{2}$
2.	-1	2.5
3.	6	5
4.	7	all
5.	10	null

6. $\geq$
7. $\leq$
8. $h < -72$

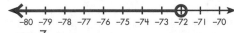

9. $a > 7$

Check What You Know, page 65

10. $\$49.23 + n \leq \$200$; $n \leq \$150.77$
11. $\$325.54 + n - \$125.43 \geq \$300$; $n \geq \$99.89$
12. $8 > z$
13. $g < -19$
14. $d < 12$
15. $13 > k$
16. $x > -17$
17. $y < -17$
18. $0 \leq r$
19. $w \geq 3$

Lesson 7.1, page 66

	a	b
1.	1	20
2.	$-\frac{3}{4}$	2
3.	$\frac{1}{5}$	2
4.	-3	50
5.	7	9
6.	4	7.1

7. $3x + 5 = 10 + x$; $2\frac{1}{2}$
8. $6 + \frac{x}{2} = 2x$; 4

Algebra Answers

Lesson 7.2, page 67

	a	b
1.	2	8
2.	all	−7
3.	4	null
4.	3	2
5.	all	$-\frac{1}{2}$
6.	null	1

Lesson 7.3, page 68

1. $\geq$
2. $\leq$
3. $\geq$
4. $\leq$
5. $x \leq 2$
6. $x \geq 32$

Lesson 7.4, page 69

1. $x < 2$

2. $t > 5$

3. $-1 < k$

4. $1 > k$

5. $n + \$16.50 \leq \$25; n \leq \$8.50$
6. $n + 1.25 > 3.5; n > 2.25$

Lesson 7.5, page 70

1. $3 \leq n$

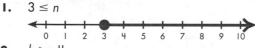

2. $h > -4$

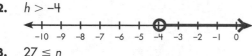

3. $27 \leq n$

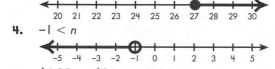

4. $-1 < n$

5. $\$6.25n \leq \$26; n \leq 4.16$
6. $4n \geq \$200; n \geq \$50$

Lesson 7.6, page 71

1. $x > -6$

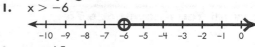

2. $z \leq 15$

3. $m \geq -9$

4. $y < 1.25$

5. $\$0.99n + \$14 \leq \$20; n \leq 6$
6. $\$8n - \$16 \geq \$200; n \geq 27$

Lesson 7.7, page 72

	a	b
1.	$x = 5$	no solution
2.	infinitely many	$z = 5$
3.	infinitely many	$c = 2.5$
4.	infinitely many	no solution
5.	$t = -3$	$d = 2$
6.	no solution	$x = 3.5$

Check What You Learned, page 73

	a	b
1.	3	0.7
2.	16	−9
3.	$\frac{1}{8}$	2
4.	0.7	all
5.	null	11
6.	$\geq$	
7.	$\geq$	
8.	$10 > z$	

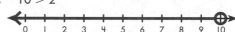

9. The solution is $x \geq 5$, so any number greater than or equal to 5 is the solution. There are an infinite number of values in the solution.

Check What You Learned, page 74

	a	b	c
10.	$b < 27$	$k > 13$	$p > 16$
11.	$n \leq 5$	$y < 36$	$x \geq 3.5$
12.	$a < 7$	$c \leq -12$	$t \geq 22$
13.	$d > -3$	$g < 16$	$y < 3$
14.	$x \geq 2$	$n \geq 16$	$k < 4$
15.	$p > 0.1$	$a \leq 21\%$	$b < -2$
16.	$\$0.85n \leq \$35; n \leq 41$		
17.	$1.25 + n \leq 4.5; n \leq 3.25$		

Algebra Answers

Chapter 8

Check What You Know, page 75

1a. Answers may vary.

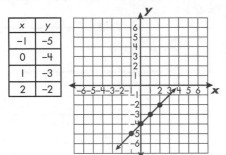

x	y
−1	−5
0	−4
1	−3
2	−2

1b. Answers may vary.

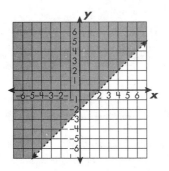

x	y
−1	−2
0	1
1	4
2	7

2a.

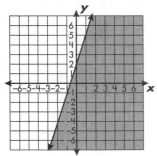

2b.

3. 3

4. 40

5. $d = 7.5t$

6. 45 minutes

Check What You Know, page 76

7. $y = 3x + 2$

8. $y = 2x − 3$

9. $y = x + 5$

10. $y = 2x − 3$

11a.   **11b.**

12. $1\frac{1}{2}$ 5

Lesson 8.1, page 77

	a		**b**		**c**	
	x	y	x	y	x	y
1.	0	−3	−2	−6	−3	−10
	1	−2	−1	−2	−2	−7
	2	−1	0	2	−1	−4
	3	0	1	6	0	−1
	4	1	2	10	1	2
	5	2	3	14	2	5
2.	x	y	x	y	x	y
	−2	−1	−8	0	−9	−4
	0	0	−4	1	−6	−3
	2	1	0	2	−3	−2
	4	2	4	3	0	−1
	6	3	8	4	3	0
	8	4	12	5	6	1
3.	x	y	x	y	x	y
	0	5	0	−1	−5	−2
	1	6	1	1	−3	−1
	2	9	2	7	−1	0
	3	14	3	17	1	1
	4	21	4	31	3	2
	5	30	5	49	5	3

Algebra Answers

Lesson 8.2, page 78

1a.

x	y
−1	2
0	3
1	4
2	5

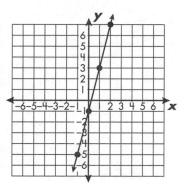

1b.

x	y
−1	−5
0	−1
1	3
2	7

2a.

x	y
−2	−2
0	−1
2	0
4	1

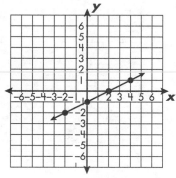

2b.

x	y
−3	−2
0	−1
3	0
6	1

Lesson 8.3, page 79

	a	b	c
1.	2; 3	3; 2	1; −2
2a.	fixed cost		
2b.	variable cost		

Lesson 8.4, page 80

Answers may vary.

	a	b
1.	1; 2	2; 1
	2; 4	4; 2
	$\frac{1}{2} = \frac{2}{4}$	$\frac{2}{4} = \frac{1}{2}$
2.	2; 3	3; 2
	4; 6	6; 4
	$\frac{2}{4} = \frac{3}{6}$	$\frac{3}{6} = \frac{2}{4}$

Lesson 8.5, page 81

1. 4
2. 15
3a. 200 (km/hour)
3b. $d = 200t$
3c. $1\frac{1}{2}$ hours
4. 5

Lesson 8.6, page 82

1. $y = 2x + 1$
2. $y = x - 2$
3. $y = \frac{x}{2} + 6$
4. $y = 2x + 5$
5. $y = x - 7$
6. $y = 2x + 2$

Lesson 8.7, page 83

1. (0, 4)   2. (−2, −4)

Lesson 8.8, page 84

	a	b
1.	$y = \frac{5}{9}x - 4$	$y = -\frac{2}{3}x - 3$
2.	$y = \frac{1}{4}x + 3$	$y = -\frac{5}{3}x - 2$

Lesson 8.9, page 85

Answers may vary.

1. The biggest increase in visitors was between months 2 and 3. The number of visitors was at its greatest at month 5. The number of visitors increased until month 5 and then decreased.

2. Grace learned words quickly in the first weeks. Grace learned fewer new words as time increased. By the end of her studying period, Grace was learning very few new words.

3. The trip began and ended at a slow rate. The family stopped moving during the middle of the trip. The family moved quicker just before the middle stop.

Algebra Answers

Lesson 8.10, page 86

1.

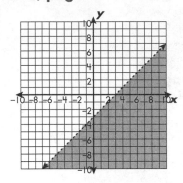

2.

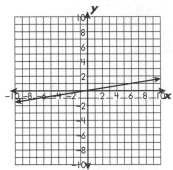

Lesson 8.11, page 87

	a	b	c
1.	yes	yes	no

2.

y
−4
4
6
9
11
14

y
−2
−1
1
3
6
8

y
−7
−5
−2
0
3
8

Lesson 8.12, page 88

	a	b
1.	$1; 2; y = \frac{1}{12}x$	$5; 8; y = x + 3$
2.	$\frac{3}{5}; \frac{3}{5};$ linear	$\frac{7}{4}; \frac{7}{4};$ linear

Lesson 8.13, page 89

	a	b	c
1.	$y = 3x$	$y = \frac{1}{3}x$	$y = 6x$
2.	$y = 2x - 2$	$y = \frac{3}{2}x - 2$	$y = x - 8$
3.	$y = x - 3$	$y = 4x - 1$	$y = 2x + 6$

Lesson 8.14, page 90

	a	b
1.	table	equation
2.	equation	table
3.	table	equation
4.	equation	equation

Check What You Learned, page 91

Answers may vary.

1a.

x	y
−1	3
0	4
1	5
2	6

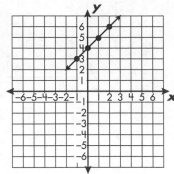

1b.

x	y
−1	−6
0	−2
1	2
2	6

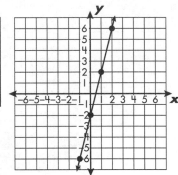

2a.

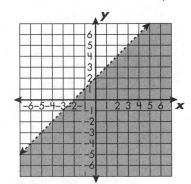

2b.

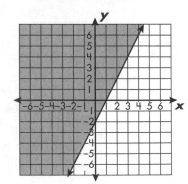

3. 2.5

4. 7

5. 24

Algebra Answers

Check What You Learned, page 92

6. $d = 16t$
7. $1\frac{1}{2}$ hours
8. $y = 4x + 2$
9. $y = x + 4$
10. $y = x - 5$
11. $y = 2x + 4$

	a	b
12.	1; 5	2; 3
	2; 10	4; 6
	$\frac{1}{2} = \frac{5}{10}$	$\frac{2}{4} = \frac{3}{6}$

Check What You Learned; page 93

	a	b	c
13.	no	yes	yes

	a	b
14.	31; 85; $y = 9x + 4$	4; 5; $y = \frac{1}{7}x - 5$
15.	−2; 2; nonlinear	6; 6; linear
16.	equation	

Chapter 9

Check What You Know, page 94

	a	b
1.	8; −1	0; −2
2.	1; −2	−6; 0

3.

0; 3   4; 2

4. $b + c = 80$; $2b + 4c = 270$; 25; 55

Check What You Know, page 95

	a	b	c
5.	−3; −6	−5; 9	3; −3

6.   7.

	a	b
8.	$-\frac{1}{2}$; $3\frac{1}{2}$	9; 5
9.	4; 3	4; 1

Lesson 9.1, page 96

	a	b
1.	yes	no
2.	no	yes

Lesson 9.2, page 97

	a	b
1.	3; 2	4; 5
2.	−3; −7	0; −5
3.	3; −3	2; 5

Lesson 9.2, page 98

	a	b
1.	6; −6	7; −1
2.	10; −1	−1; −1
3.	−1; 3	−1; −8

Lesson 9.3, page 99

	a	b
1.		

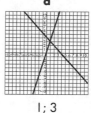

1; 3   2; 8

2.

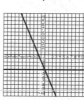

0; −4   −1; −4

Lesson 9.3, page 100

1.

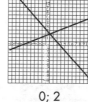

0; 2   1; 4

2.

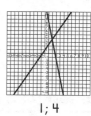

−2; −4   5; 1

Lesson 9.4, page 101

1. $w + s = 172$; $(\$1.10)w + (\$2.35)s = \$294.20$; 88; 84
2. $t + f = 40$; $2t + 4f = 100$; 30; 10

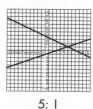

Algebra Answers

Check What You Learned, page 102

	a	b
1.	−1; −5	8; 10
2.	−6; 4	2; 0

3.

−5; 1   −5; 7

4. $t + x = 15; 2t + 3x = 33; 12; 3$

Check What You Learned, page 103

5. $c + a = 2,200; 1.50c + 4a = 5,050; 1,500; 700$

	a	b	c
6.	4; 16	16; 5	10; 16

7.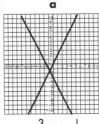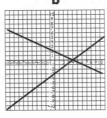

$-\frac{3}{4}; -1\frac{1}{2}$ 4; 0

Final Test (Chapters 1–9), page 104

1. $18x + 18$
2. $250 + 500c$
3. $\frac{2x}{3}$
4. $5\frac{7}{12}$ hours
5. \$0.83 or $\frac{29}{35}$ of a dollar
6. $\$1.50 \times p \leq \$22.00$; 14
7. $n + (n + 1) + (n + 2) = 51$; 16
8. $(p + 5) \div 2 = 16$; 27

Final Test (Chapters 1–9), page 105

	a	b	c
9.	−5.5	48	11

	a	b
10.	2	4
11.	17	all
12.	11	null

13. $\$15 \times 3 + 5\% (\$15 \times 3) = n$; \$47.25
14. $\$250 + \$5n \leq \$320$; $n \leq 14$
15. $y = 8x − 34$
16. $y = x + 10$

	a	b
17.	3^1	8^{-3}
18.	2^{-2}	4^6

Final Test (Chapters 1–9), page 106

19a.

x	y
−8	−3
−4	−1
0	1
6	4

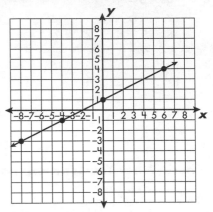

19b.

x	y
−2	−8
0	−4
3	2
5	6

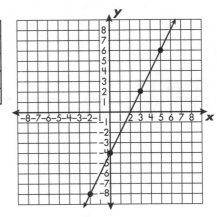

20. $d = 3.5t$

21.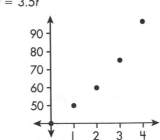

22. $(−4,−1); (−1,−1); (−1, −5)$
23. $(0,4); (3,4); (3, 0)$

Final Test (Chapters 1–9), page 107

24. 5 in.; 7.5 in.

	a	b
25.	9; 1	−1; −2
26.	1; 3	5; 6

27. $q + d = 57$; $(\$0.25)q + (\$0.10)d = \$12.00$; 42; 15

28. 1; 3   2; 2
    2; 6   6; 6
    $\frac{1}{2} = \frac{3}{6}$ $\frac{2}{6} = \frac{2}{6}$